CLASSROOM TIME MANAGEMENT

BOOK III: ORGANIZING WORK

Revised Edition

Dick Webster
Dave Bailey

Webley Associates, Rochester, Minnesota 55902

The editors were Dr. E. Gershon, Warren Zimmerman, and Darla Olson.
The cover was designed by Doug Case and his high school students.
Modern Press was the printer and binder.
Published by:

Webley Associates
937-7th Avenue S.W.
Rochester, MN 55902
(507) 288-8074
If no answer, call (507) 282-7834

CLASSROOM TIME MANAGEMENT

Book III: Organizing Work

ISBN 1-881449-02-5

ABOUT
THE AUTHORS

Dick Webster is presently a retired Staff Development Coordinator, K-12, from the Rochester Independent School District 535. Currently, he is on the adjunct staff for Winona State University, teaching graduate classes on "The Improvement of Instruction. "He taught physical education Pre-K through high school, directed health and physical education programs K-6 for 16 years, coordinated athletic programs K-12, and was the director of the Winona State University Graduate Induction Program for three years.

Dave Bailey is presently a Clinical Supervisor for the Winona State University Graduate Induction Program K-6. He has supervised over 30 student teachers and taught grades 6, 5, and 3. He was one of the eleven selected for the Minnesota Education Association's 1991 Teachers of Excellence. In addition, he has taught numerous staff development and college classes in the areas of Peer Coaching, Cooperative Learning, and Time Management.

BOOK III   Organizing Work

CLASSROOM TIME MANAGEMENT

Book I Organizing Self and Others

Book II Organizing Students

Book III Organizing Work

NOTE TO TEACHERS

This book is made up of many ideas which are effective to different styles of teaching. The same skill or activity may be done in a number of different ways and still be time-efficient and effective for a teacher.

The real purpose of this book is to share some of the time-efficient and effective ideas of teachers so that other teachers can use them, modify them, or brainstorm other ideas from the ones given; in order to develop better classroom time management.

There are not enough hours in the day to do all the things that <u>could</u> <u>be</u> <u>done</u> in teaching, but maybe this book will help you be more time-efficient and effective with one or two of your current practices; so that in the end, this book will have been worthwhile to you.

THESE TIMESAVING IDEAS ARE BAR-CODED: **K-2** ON **TOP ONE THIRD**, **3-4** ON **MIDDLE THIRD**, and **5-6** on **BOTTOM THIRD OF EACH PAGE**. IDEAS WHICH ARE ESPECIALLY APPLICABLE TO **ALL GRADES K-6** ARE **NOT BAR-CODED**. PLEASE BE AWARE THAT MANY OF THE IDEAS SHARED BY TEACHERS TRANSCEND ACROSS SEVERAL GRADE LEVELS. BE SURE TO READ **ALL** THE GRADES' SUGGESTIONS IN ORDER TO PROFIT FROM THE MANY OTHER EXCELLENT IDEAS.

Teachers described these timesaving ideas to us in detail. The ideas have been condensed purposefully to save your time. The main ideas are presented to you in a manner that should expedite your time. You may adapt them to your style and teaching situation.

It is our sincere wish that you will find several entries to save you time in many areas and make your profession the most enjoyable.

DEDICATION

We would like to dedicate this book to all the excellent teachers of Independent School District 535, Rochester, Minnesota, in remembrance of all their years of past, present, and future professional dedication.

From all the information received, there were three main themes that emerged over and over again from the majority of teachers interviewed. First, all of these teachers put many **extra** hours into their workday beyond the "required" time. Second, **planning**, both short- and long-range, was a very important part of their teaching schedule. Third, the use of students to do many of the daily tasks was developed through **direct teaching** of the **skills of independence** to students at grade levels K-6.

ACKNOWLEDGEMENTS

There were over one hundred teachers who made this book possible. The first group of teachers, who provided their expertise and ideas, are listed on the next page.

The second group of teachers, who shared their expertise and ideas, wished not to have their names listed.

The last group of teachers are those who were not asked to share their ideas due to time restrictions, but would have shared their ideas if asked.

A special "Thank You" to Warren Zimmerman, retired Elementary Principal, who assisted with the writing of the introductions to each chapter.

CLARIFICATION: Teachers were selected, by their grade levels (K-6), at each building, thus providing a mixture of teaching experiences.

Any errors in interpretations of the information given by teachers is unintentional.

TEACHERS CREDITED

Holly Anderson	Darlene Forbrook	Gloria Obermeyer
Joyce Anderson	Kathleen Freeberg	Herbert Ollenburg
Peggy Anderson	Bob Gray	Marlys Ostby
Sue Bock (Greenberg)	Bonnie Gunderson	Carol Passi
Ramona Back	Charles Healy	Bill O'Reilly
Bonnie Bailey	Diane Kinneberg	Linda Rud
Kim Benda	Kelly Kosidowski	Esther Schmidt
Bruce Bigelow	Jim Kulzer	Carol Schroedel
Barbara Campbell	Dorette Leimer	Phillip Settell
Janet Carstensen	Leo Loosbrock	Gwen Stanich
Rosemary Chafos	Scott Mahle	Joe Stanich
Jane Coy	Marilyn McKeehen	Bill Temple
Lois Crouch	Mary Beth Miller	Dorie Thamert
Betty Danielson	Nancy Mix	Tom Theismann
Char Davis	Evelyn Nauman	Arlene Thone
Joan Davis	Don Nelson	Lynn Tollar
Doris DeSart	Marilyn Norland	Jay VanOort
Tony Floyd		

Chapter I - Directions

INTRODUCTION

You will save time if directions are presented in the correct manner, remembering that students learn in different modalities: audio, visual, and tactile.

Directions need to be clear, sequential, and appropriate to the student's ability level. As a result you should not have to repeat directions; students won't miss details, and you won't feel rushed. You and your students will feel positive with the results.

GENERAL SUGGESTIONS

Being able to clearly give directions that **all** students can understand and follow will build a feeling of competence for students. Also, it can provide for increased time on task as well as facilitate classroom management.

There are three main reasons why students **do not** follow directions:
1. The student does not intend to follow directions.
2. The student is incapable of following the directions.
3. The directions themselves, or methods of giving directions, has power to confuse or make unclear.

Reasons two and three indicate a change must be made by the teacher so he/she applies what is known about learning to the achievement of direction following.

In the first two situations the teacher must address the following two questions:
1. Is the student really trying to follow the directions?
2. Is the student able to follow the directions if he/she tries?

The third questions can be addressed very directly.
1. Are your students taught directions or do you assume they understand directions.

(Directions)

There are two basic steps to follow whenever you want to give clear directions to students.

STEP I - Planning

1. **HOW MANY** directions can you give at one time?
   - no more than three oral directions at one time without a written reference
   - secondary dependent upon training previously provided
   - introduce only **one new** direction at a time
   - complex behaviors can be broken into several sets of directions with one set being accomplished before the next set is given

2. **WHEN** do you give directions?
   - as close to the time of execution as possible
   - give **all** the directions before having students move
   - hand out papers (materials) after directions are given

3. **WHAT** information?
   - include information of who does what by when
   - give the directions in the order to be carried out

STEP II - Giving Directions (individual or group)

1. Gain the attention of **all** students for whom the directions are intended. Have the students focus on the teacher who is giving the directions. (This is one of the main causes of confused or unclear directions received by students.)

2. Give the directions as planned in the correct sequence.

3. Check for understanding. Unfortunately giving directions **well** does not guarantee they have been understood. When the teacher checks for understanding, he/she should make it clear that students are accountable for listening and following directions. The teacher could ask appropriate questions such as "What's the first thing you'll do?"

4. Model the behavior **when appropriate**. Modeling is effective for the students who learn best by seeing. Also, other students will benefit by attending consciously to the modeling.

5. Let the students begin. The teacher must decide if all students, or a few at a time, will proceed. The class **should not be held** up for one or two students who may need additional individual help.

RESOURCES

1. Hunter, Dr. Madeline, Improved Instruction: Take 10 Staff Meetings as Directed, El Segundo, CA. TIP Publications, 1976.
2. ISD #535, Staff Development Handbook, pp.173-174, 1987.

TEACH LISTENING

Teach listening skills. Simon Says, Telephone, SRA Listening Skills Tapes, etc. taught during the first few weeks of school help set the focus for better direction following.

USE MODALITIES

Use different modalities to enhance directions. Tell them, show them, by modeling what they are to accomplish, perhaps draw pictures of each step. Quantify the steps by having the student count the steps and name each one as they touch their fingers (**1.** turn on water, **2.** wash hands, **3.** dry with towel, **4.** throw towel in basket.)

CHECKING FOR UNDERSTANDING

Follow the Madeline Hunter Lesson Plan Steps, concentrating on the "Checking for Understanding." They must **all** be ready to give feedback on the directions. Check their auditory and visual memories. What did they see and hear? Use print, pictures, and peers to reinforce your directions first. Clarify any misconceptions before starting the project.

NUMBERED SEQUENCE

Try to sit where all the students are near you. Give directions by quantifying them by number of events sequenced. First, second, third, etc. Draw sequence in picture form as well as verbal explanation.

"Always have a reason for whatever you do."

Marlys Ostby

NOTES:

"Our children may go wrong if we don't start them

right."

Anonymous

CHALKBOARD Write the directions on the board or have students copy them in a personal assignment book. You'll integrate reading, writing, and higher level thinking skills through accountability.

STUDENT ASSIGN-MENT BOOK Encourage responsibility by having the students write directions and assignments in their personal assignment books along with the date due. Then they will have them even when doing the work at home or in another room.

LONG-TERM DIRECTION Write any long-term directions down and tape them on the work folder, bulletin board, station area, etc. Cover them with plastic transparency contact paper, or laminate them for durability and reuse. The "rule of thumb" is to write down any directions with more than three steps of **new** expectations. **(See example "A", p. 11)**

SIGNAL FIRST Have a signal to proceed the actual directions. Give the directions only once. Put multiple directions in writing on the board. Signals may be "Eyes on me," "Time!," all raise their hands when you do, flick off the light switch, etc..

TIME SAVER Give directions before going to the gym. You won't have to go through the work of quieting them down to begin in the gym. Also, give the next room directions before you leave the gym.

STUDENTS READ Cut down on teacher talk by having the **students read** the directions. Rotate from student to student and orally to silent. Be sure to check for understanding by having them repeat the directions in their own words.

UNDERLINE DIRECTIONS When dealing with written directions, have the students underline, circle key words, or ideas in the directions. This helps to focus on the essentials. Key words may also be put on the chalkboard.

COOPERATIVE GROUPS Assign roles of "reader" and "task person" in cooperative groups. The reader reads all the directions and the task person is responsible for answering any questions the rest of the group has about the directions. This elicits purposeful listening and more involvement through positive interdependence.

TOTAL PICTURE   Share the week's schedule with the students. Fill in a blank schedule with the class on Monday morning. They will be better able to manage themselves if they know the total picture. **(See example "B", p. 12)**

".....What isn't tried, won't work. --

Claude McDonald in The Christian World

ASSIGNMENTS ON TOP OF PAPERS

Have students write all assignments and directions on the top of their papers so they aren't forgotten. It serves as a proofreading exercise to make sure they've included everything. Have them check off the steps as they go.

ESTABLISH PROCEDURE EARLY

Really work on your presentations at the start of the year. Set a tone for the whole year right from the beginning. Give directions only once and have high expectations for listening and for asking questions at the appropriate time. These efforts will be worth it!

VISUAL CLUES

Write directions so students can see directions many times. Use the chalkboard, overhead, and on their papers. State them very clearly and specifically. Don't give verbal directions until all eyes are looking at you and there is no talking.

"One may go wrong in many different directions but right in only one."

Anonymous

BEFORE YOU BEGIN Before giving any directions, have all the students put their names and headings on their papers and look up. This eliminates writing while you're giving important directions.

100% FOCUS One signal to use prior to giving directions would be a silent pause to be sure you have 100% body and eye readiness.

"ECHO" Require all eyes on the teacher when giving directions. randomly select a student to "echo" the directions back for the class. This encourages better listening.

NEVER REPEAT DIRECTIONS Teach children to listen for directions the first time by making it your policy never to repeat directions yourself. If they need help, the natural consequence would be that they seek the information from another student, or reread the written ones.

STUDENT REPEATS DIRECTIONS If repeats are necessary, students, not the teacher, should repeat them. These can be repeated to the class, or better yet, tell the student to check quietly with an "on-task" student so as not to disturb the whole class.

TRANSFER AN IDEA When teaching how to listen for directions, compare it to watching television. You sit still, eliminate everything else, and listen "intently." Children can identify with this model.

ASK QUESTIONS OF STUDENTS Don't just repeat the directions for them. Students become dependent if they know they can just ask for a repeat. Instead, ask them questions such as: "What don't you understand?", "What were the directions?", or "What do you think you should do?" This forces them to think for themselves and sets a tone to listen better the first time.

DEVELOP A ROUTINE Establish a routine of not repeating any directions for the first five minutes of individual practice. This encourages better listening and gets the questions out of the way before the class begins work on their own.

CHECK FOR UNDERSTANDING Check for understanding by having a student repeat your directions back for the class before anyone starts. Students listen better to peers, and they have the knack for explaining it in a child's vocabulary.

ASK, "WHY" Increase thinking skills and understanding by asking," WHY? What is this part of the direction for? Why do it in this order? What is the purpose?" Bloom's Taxonomy is integrated in.

MODEL Whenever possible, try to model by having students do one example all together. They all follow the same set of directions at once. This involves them and they can learn from each other before they try to do it individually.

CHECKLIST For those students who have great difficulty following a sequence of directions, write them out, and have a place in front of each step to be checked off before the next step is started.

COOPERATIVE GROUPS Make it a rule in cooperative groups that all members must raise their hands before you help them with directions. This forces them to ask each other before relying on the teacher.

STANDARD PROCEDURE Establish a standard procedure for students to follow whenever they complete their assigned work. Teach this early in the school year. **How** to collect papers, **where** are they put, **when** to turn them in, **who** collects them, **what** is collected, and **why** do you do it this way. Have an "assignment folder" in each child's desk so they don't get lost. Collecting the assignments all at once eliminates the excuse of "I already handed that in."

STEPS ON CHALKBOARD Put your directions on the chalkboard, list them in order, answer any questions, and let the students go on their own. They just check the chalkboard if they forget a step and to affirm what they've already done. Less teacher contact time is the goal to encourage self-directed learners and responsibility.

ANTICIPATION Anticipate concerns and problems. Experience helps with this, but one can always think ahead. The more specific you can be, the more self-directed you can expect the students to be. This saves time in the long run.

MODEL Model directions after they are given. Do an example together before the students go on to independent practice. A visual is worth a thousand words.

SPELLING:

* Record scores on green spelling record cards

* Fill out yellow home reports

* File tests in order

* File returned yellow home reports

* Put yellow home reports in _____

INVENTORY:

SAVE for home

SPELLING:

* Record scores on green spelling record cards

* Fill out yellow home reports

* File tests in order

* File returned yellow home reports

* Put yellow home reports in _____

INVENTORY:

SAVE for home

SPELLING

* Record scores on green spelling record cards

* Fill out yellow home reports

* File tests in order

* File returned yellow home reports

* Put yellow home reports in _____

INVENTORY:

SAVE for home

SPELLING

* Record scores on green spelling record cards

* Fill out yellow home reports

* File tests in order

* File returned yellow home reports

* Put yellow home reports in _____

INVENTORY:

SAVE for home

NAME _____

Time		MONDAY	TUESDAY	WEDNESDAY	THURSDAY	FRIDAY
8:45	Attendance					
9:00	Journal					
10:10	Break					
10:25						
10:50 11:15	P.E.					
11:45						
12:05	Lunch					
12:55	Relaxation/ story					
1:10						
2:00						
2:50	Evaluation & dismissal					

12

Chapter II - Assignments

| **TEACHER PLEASE NOTE:** | Please be aware that many of the ideas shared by teachers can and do transcend across several grade levels. Be sure to read all grades' suggestions in order to profit from the many other excellent ideas. |

INTRODUCTION

Students tend to live up to (or down to) your expectations. Assignments are no different. Set your standards high. Following through with appropriate instruction, and constancy right from the start, will save you lots of time and anxiety later.

A few students may need a special, individualized plan, including parent involvement until, they assume their responsibilies.

Good planning and early instruction in this area will yield more completed assignments and less time spent following up by the teacher.

NOTES:

"Ask three before me."

unknown

ORGANIZE "POCKET"

For daily assignments, have a tagboard pocket attached to the side of the student's desk. All work assignments go in there for the day. It helps to keep the desk top free and the inside not so messy. It is a visual check for you to see who is finished and who is behind, depending on how much is sticking up.

WEEKEND READING ASSIGNMENT

Every weekend, have students take home their reading books and read to their parent(s) using homework charts. The parent signs the work chart and sends it back with the book on Monday.

STUDENT FOLDER

Teach organization with a folder. Each student has his/her name on a same colored folder. Work to be done goes in the left side, and work completed goes in the right side. You do not have to sort papers, and if the name is forgotten, you still know whose it is.

KEEPING FOCUS

Have students come up and sit in front of you while giving directions. This encourages good listening and prevents those "fast starters" from getting away from you. You will only have to answer the clarifying question one time as opposed to separate questions later on.

MARKING PEN REMINDERS

Try putting a marking pen dot on the back of the children's hand as a reminder for a homework assignment due the next day. Parents are informed of the meaning, and it only takes a minute to walk down the aisle to give the dots to students.

STUDENT CHECKING OFF

The first student finished with an assignment is responsible for taking a class list and checking off the rest of the class as they turn in their papers. This goes on top of that assignment's pile as a quick check for you to see who is missing. They can even be put in alphabetical order. **(See example "P", p. 48)**

ELIMINATE EXCUSES

To eliminate excuses for not getting work done on time, let students come into the room before the bell for a study period. It will show you that they care. Encourage only those who NEED this opportunity.

CHECKING OFF ASSIGNMENTS

When students write down the assignments in their notebooks, or assignment books, have them make a small box in front of their assignment. They check off the boxes when completed. It is a visual and self-rewarding for the student. It eliminates messy scratching and scribbling, and allows for checking back to see what still needs to be done.

USING A STAMP

Make up a stamp and inform parents of its meaning. If parents see this at the top of a paper, it signals "EXTRA IMPORTANT." It is used for homework to be done, redos, or make-up work.

CHRONIC LATE ASSIGNMENTS

For the chronic late assignments, set up a daily note to go home which must be signed by the parent or guardian and returned the following day. Make this a few weeks commitment and then let them try their wings again. The child shouldn't become dependent on it, but gain awareness. **(See example "C", p. 27)**

VISUAL HELP

Use a cardboard clock to show a "delinquent" student when his/her assignments should be finished. This concrete visual helps the student to be more conscious of time. Tape the clock to the student's desk.

PARENT/CHILD ACTIVITY

Assign parent/child activities for homework. For example, let each child select an animal book. Each takes it home and reads it to his/her parents. Afterwards, he/she prints a story following an outline. **(See example "N", p. 42)** It is best to give the parents an instructional sheet regarding the project ahead of time, or put it in a newsletter.

WORK CHART

Have students take home their reading books and read to their parents every weekend. The parent signs a "Work Chart" and sends it back with the student on Monday.

COLOR CODE

Color code everything for each group. Their folders, book edges, notebooks, etc. are so much faster to collect and hand out if they can be spotted quickly. If something gets into the wrong group's pile, it is easily retrieved without looking through everything. It is a quick way to identify which group a student is in and that can make a difference in your expectations.

STUDENTS WRITE THEIR ASSIGNMENT(S)

Use scrap paper (8 1/2 x 11) cut in fourths for students to write their day's assignment. Work not crossed off, as completed, goes home as homework. Parents know the procedure and check their child's list each night. It also indicates what was done during the day.

MODELING AND PRIORITIZING

Teach good study skills and work habits by modeling assignments on the board and prioritizing them. Do this for one half the school year, and then expect the students to do it themselves with personal assignment books the rest of the year.

STUDENTS WITH A PROBLEM

Use assignment sheets for students with problems getting work done on time. Simply glue this small form sheet to their desks with rubber cement. It comes off easily. Students are responsible for filling it in. The teacher signs it off with initials if done on time. The record provides data for conferences, or to send as a note for parent/guardian. The prominence and visibility make it hard for the student to forget. **(See example "A", p. 25)**

LIBRARY POCKETS

Have library pockets on the side of students' desks. Students fill in a short form for assignments to do, and keep it there. For students who have problems with completing their work on a chronic basis, color code for extra help and incentive. Parent involvement might be warranted, in which case, yet another color could be used to send home for a signature each night.

SELF-DIRECTED STUDENTS

Make out a chapter outline with assignments for individualized, self-directed students. Include a place to record scores. Hold individual conferences regularly. Make chapter outlines nice enough to use year after year.

MONTHS' ASSIGNMENT(S)

Give assignments for the month. Keep their work in their folders until they are completed. It is easy to individualize instruction by adding or subtracting from the folders during periodic reviews.

REVIEW TIME

Set aside time each month to review assignments given for the month. Major concepts, self-evaluation of effort, spelling words missed; samples of all major concepts are reinforced with a short assignment. Parents enjoy seeing these, and it gives an easy, regular update, in-between grading periods.

STRIPS OF PAPER
Use up scrap paper by cutting up into strips. Each morning each student picks up a strip and a piece of tape at the door. They record each assignment as given and cross out when completed. Anything not completed becomes homework. Write any special notices, such as book order, conference slips due, materials needed, etc. on the bottom of the strip at the end of the day. It eliminates assignment books and is always in sight for the teacher to check on or add to. A student partner can easily keep track of assignments for absentee students, too.

CHALKBOARD AND COLORED PAPER
Put reading group names on the chalkboard with colored paper. It is easy to distinguish and their particular assignments are written next to the name. Like colored folders are keyed into the program for the teacher's ease of collecting and returning work.

MUST COMPLETE WORK
Work not completed on time **must** be done during breaks, at noon, or before going home. This high expectation, followed through on early in the year, will prevent a lot of problems later. It is worth the time spent.

WRITE DOWN INSTRUCTIONS
During whole class instruction (versus Cooperative Learning Groups) always write down the instructions if there are more than three new, unfamiliar directions to be followed.

BEING IMPORTANT
Don't assign anything unless it is important enough to be expected to be done and followed up on to ensure it is. Students can recognize "busy work."

CHRONIC LATE ASSIGNMENTS
For chronic late assignments, establish a daily homework sheet. The parent makes a slash one way when complete (/) and you complete the (X) when you agree. Teamwork equals accountability and results.

STUDENTS WHO DO NOT COMPLETE WORK
Students who do not complete an assignment have their name(s) put on the chalkboard. If the work is not completed that day, they receive a check after their name and a note goes home to the parents. This can be adapted to a form, filled in by the teacher and signed by the parent to be returned the following day. If not returned, a follow-up phone call is in order.

POST IT STICKY
Use a Post-it sticky for each assignment not finished. These are put on the student's desk. This gives you a visual pulse to monitor a problem-child's progress.

TWO DAYS' MAKEUP
Allow two days to make up each day's absence within which to get all their makeup work finished and to keep up with the new material.

NO HOMEWORK POLICY
Prevent parent/guardian from calling or visiting at at inappropriate times for homework by establishing the policy of : "NO HOMEWORK given until the child returns from being gone." If several students are absent, it takes a long time individually to get all the work together with textbooks and assignments. If the student is sick, he/she needs the rest and not to be pushed to do homework before feeling better. Use a makeup sheet and give the assignments to the student upon his/her return to the classroom.

NOTEBOOK INFORMATION
Have students write page numbers, due date, and special instructions on top of the notebook page or loose-leaf paper they will be using to complete the assignment. They will have it there if they need to take it home and it promotes responsibility.

SUBJECT AREA NOTEBOOKS
Students do their homework in **Subject-area** notebooks. There are no loose papers to loose; it is a complete record to review anytime during the year and provides an excellent reference during parent/teacher/child conferences. Put a generic form on the inside cover of each notebook.
(See example "D", p. 28)

PLAY ASSIGNMENT
Whenever you do a play, assign two sets of characters. This way there will be maximum participation, and if someone is absent for the final performance, there will be an immediate "understudy" to take his/her place.

VIDEO VS. MAKEUP
Every few weeks, team with another teacher to show a video to those who have all their assignments done. Take turns monitoring the video and overseeing the study period group. Announce the video and restrictions a week ahead. Don't have a set schedule for videos.

CHOICES
Give students some choices and a feeling of control over their learning. Hook them in by asking, (for example: "Which five problems do you want to do besides the problems 1, 10, and 25?").

NOTES:

"What we have to learn to do, we learn by doing."

Aristotle

GAUGE THE AMOUNT
Gauge the amount of independent practice to the "average" student. Decrease the amount for slower students or allow more homework time, too. Give extension activities to use independent time for the faster finishers.

NO WEEKEND HOMEWORK
Do not schedule homework for the weekend. Students need their time too. Encourage students to openly discuss why we have assignments; the importance, positives and negatives.

SELF-RESPONSIBILITY
Check in assignments, and keep the lists readily available for the students to check to see if they have everything in. Self-responsibility means you don't have to do so much verbal reminding.

"3-STRIKE" RULE
Create a "3-strike" rule. If a student misses three assignments within a quarter, he/she must complete any further assignments before going home each day. Parents are notified, and the slate is wiped clean at the end of each quarter.

CHALKBOARD
Put all assignments on large chalkboards for a week ahead. As each is completed by the entire class or group, it is erased. Have separate "Head Start" assignments for students who complete their work for the week and have additional time.

POST AHEAD
Build toward success. Post ahead of time all tests to be given and the major items and skills to be covered. There should be no hidden, trick agendas.

REWARDS POINT SYSTEM
Give group points for assignments being in on time. Assign groups for two weeks at a time. Peer pressure in reminding each other to get names on papers and assignments in on time saves on teacher input time. Give one point for name and one point for being in on time. Students can keep their own scores. Points can be used for perks after two weeks. One child can be put out of the group after three problems and if the rest of the group presents a tactful case to the teacher. Points could also be given for additional positive behaviors.

**ESTABLISH
RULE**

Discuss and establish a rule at the beginning of the year:
**Assignments must be done on time or the consequence
Is a 'O' for that assignment. Assignments must then
complete an action plan of 50 words or more telling what
they are going to do to get them in on time in the future.
Three zeros and a contact with the parent/guardian is
made for a conference."**

**INDIVIDUAL
ASSIGNMENT
SHEET**

Use individual assignments sheets. **(See example "E", p. 29)**
Students fill them in at the beginning of each day according
to the information on the chalkboard. It saves you time telling
them any assignments that were not completed on time
during the day. They take the sheets home finished or not.
Parents are interested in seeing what is being done at school
and encourage getting work completed. Just staple the
incomplete work to the individual assignment sheet.

**EXTRA WORK
PROJECTS**

Set up an extra work project which relates to what long-
range theme is being studied over the quarter. The parts of
the project can earn monopoly money with your name
stamped on it. At the end of the specified time period, hold
an auction with the money. Prizes can be inexpensive items
purchased with PTSA funds.

*"There is never enough time to do all the things
that could or should be done."*

LaVonne Ryberg

DAY'S ASSIGNMENT
Write the day's assignment on the board before school starts that day. They will be there for the student who is out of the room, and it saves you the time of doing it during "the heat of the battle."

BULLETIN BOARD
Set up an Assignment Bulletin Board. Have a large sheet of newsprint for each subject. Students have turns writing assignments and due dates on the proper sheet. Aren't sure, just check the board!

ORDER TO BE DONE
Tape up all worksheets, in the order to be completed, under a heading **"ASSIGNMENTS FOR TODAY."** This is an easy visual for students to check on themselves.

PARENT(S) INVOLVED
Reemphasize assignments through your newsletters. Many children do not share requirements at home. Get parents involved. Give ideas for extension ideas. This helps with high potential requests and gives them something better to do than watch television.

REUSE
Carefully plan out unit contracts or assignments to be sent home. Reuse them each year with only minor revisions needed. Time spent up front is time banked for later.
(See example "F", p. 30)

USE OF A CALENDAR
Write down due dates on a large calendar or on the board for easy student and teacher reference. This allows the students some choice of how to plan their time and they get a good feeling of being more independent. No one likes nagging, verbal reminders.

REVIEW ASSIGNMENTS
Give review assignments from time to time. This cements retention, adding to the student's long term memory. Perhaps assign it as homework. Regardless, don't depend upon covering the material once and presuming it is mastered for the future.

NOTES:

"*Nothing ventured, nothing gained.*"

Proverb

Date

Work to be done:

☐ ☐ ☐ ☐ ☐ ☐

Date

Work to be done:

☐ ☐ ☐ ☐ ☐ ☐

INTERMEDIATE MAKE-UP SLIP

Student Name_____ Date(s) Absent_____

___SUBJECT_____ DATE DUE   TEACHER INITIALS

_____

_____

_____

_____

_____

_____

_____

_____

Return to home classroom teacher upon completion.

INTERMEDIATE MAKE-UP SLIP

Student Name_____ Date(s) Absent_____

___SUBJECT_____ DATE DUE   TEACHER INITIAL

_____

_____

_____

_____

_____

_____

_____

Return to home classroom teacher upon completion.

	M	T	W	Th	Fri
Math					
Language					
Reading					
Writing					
Short Shots					
PIC					

_____
Parent signature

	M	T	W	Th	Fri
Math					
Language					
Reading					
Writing					
Short Shots					
PIC					

_____
Parent signature

	M	T	W	Th	Fri
Math					
Language					
Reading					
Writing					
Short Shots					
PIC					

_____
Parent signature

	M	T	W	Th	Fri
Math					
Language					
Reading					
Writing					
Short Shots					
PIC					

_____
Parent signature

Name _____

Monday	Tuesday	Wednesday	Thursday	Friday

1
2
3
4
5

1
2
3
4
5

ASSIGNMENT SHEET

Date _____

Assignment Completed   Teacher Initials

Spelling _____   Yes _____ No _____   _____

Language _____   Yes _____ No _____   _____

Math _____   Yes _____ No _____   _____

Reading _____   Yes _____ No _____   _____

Social Studies _____   Yes _____ No _____   _____

Science/Health _____   Yes _____ No _____   _____

Other _____   Yes _____ No _____   _____

_____

Teacher Comments _____

Parent Comments _____

Parent Signature _____

Name_____

Unit: Significant You

Theme: Chemicals

Assignment:

Bring in magazine or newspaper pictures of chemicals that are: 1. Safe 2. Not Safe 3. Safe (when given by a qualified adult)

You may also bring in flattened boxes or labels.

HOMEWORK NOTICE

To the Parent(s) of _____

Subject _____ Date _____

Your child did not complete the following homework assignment(s)
which was due _____
Date

_____

_____

_____

Student's signature _____

Teacher's signature _____

Please return notice to teacher the day after it is issued.

_____   _____
Parent(s) signature   Date

Comments _____

_____

31

GET IT DONE **TODAY**

Name _____

Homeroom _____

GET IT DONE **TODAY**

Name _____

Homeroom _____

GET IT DONE **TODAY**

Name _____

Homeroom _____

GET IT DONE **TODAY**

Name _____

Homeroom _____

DATE_____

Assignment	
Math	
Reading	
Language	
Spelling	
Soc. St.	
Science/ Health	
Library Reading	

DATE_____

Assignment	
Math	
Reading	
Language	
Spelling	
Soc. St.	
Science/ Health	
Library Reading	

DATE_____

Assignment	
Math	
Reading	
Language	
Spelling	
Soc. St.	
Science/ Health	
Library Reading	

DATE_____

Assignment	
Math	
Reading	
Language	
Spelling	
Soc. St.	
Science/ Health	
Library Reading	

ASSIGNMENTS FOR WEEK OF _____

NAME _____

	Reading	Math	Spelling	English	Science	Social Studies	Other
MON							
TUES							
WED							
THURS							
FRI							

34

Lizards

Weekend Homework

A New Book

We are starting our new homework chart! Did you hear about our homework present? We all got a ruler, a notepad, +a marker.

New Words

eat fish dolphin see big
whale will

wē bē shē wē hē mē
Ken Ben ten den hen men

Contractions

we'll   she'll   he'll   I'll
can't   let's   she's   he's

Stories

"Ken and the Fish" page 6
"Ana and the Whale" page 10

Phrases on the next page

Parent signature for completed homework

Auction Week   December 18-22

   Prizes will be available at 1:00 on Friday. The highest bidder gets the item up for bids. Prizes will include books, posters, pencils, candy, big pieces of art paper, fruits, unknown wrapped items, and other items I find while shopping.
   Projects have to be turned in to me by 3:30 on Thursday. Monopoly money will be given to you daily. It is your responsibility to keep your cash in a safe place.
   Each project will be worth 5, 10, 15, 20, 25 or 50 dollars.

   Here is a list of projects for bucks.
1. Show me a page-long entry in your journal. Write about being the only child, oldest child, youngest child, middle child, or second child. Tell what you like or dislike about being the child in this position. **$20**
2. You and a parent read and discuss articles in a newspaper. Look for the 5 Ws. A half hour is worth **$25**. Give me a signed slip.
3. Read a book for 20 minutes. In one good short paragraph, tell why you like or dislike a certain character. **$15**
4. Write a letter to someone. Include an envelope and stamp. **$20**
5. Fix one part of a meal. **$10**
   Fix a meal that includes all four food groups. Get comments and signatures. List what you served. **$20**
6. On Wednesday, perform a puppet play that teaches a value lesson. **$20**
7. Learn 25 hard spelling words. You create the list of words. Mastery is 88%. Have someone give you the test. **$25**
8. Draw a large map of your favorite state. Locate 10 cities. Tell why you like this state. **$10**
9. Write a thank you card to someone. **$5**
10. Sing a song in front of the class. You may be in a group. **$10**
11. Play an instrument in front of the class. Be ready on Tuesday or Thursday. **$15**
12. Demonstrate a science experiment. Be ready at 8:30 on Wednesday. **$25**
13. Perform a mime routine. Be ready at 9 on Wednesday. **$10**
14. Write and perform a humorous rap. **$20**
15. Write a book report. Use the form I gave you. **$25**
16. Do a report about the Steger expedition. **$25**
17. Illustrate each chapter of a book. Bind it in sequence. **$50**
18. Dust part of the room for 20 minutes. **$10**
19. Worksheets will be available daily. **$10**
20. Recite a poem that has 10 or more lines. **$10**

Ways to lose money:
1. Talking out of turn is **$5**.
2. Wasting time is **$5**.
3. A messy desk if **$5**.
4. Work not done is **$20**.
5. If you are not behaving after lunch is **$20**.

Day	Time Spent	Activity
Thursday		
Weekend		
Monday		
Tuesday		
Wednesday		

Week of ___Feb. 22 - March 1___

Spelling words - Review test 13-18 on Monday Feb. 26

Read a book

Test on oceans and continents on Thurs., March 1
(label on a map)

Encourage homework with a weekly tally sheet to be filled in by the parents at home. It takes little time on your part, yet it holds the student accountable and parents are included in the learning team.

37

Please return each Thursday

Day	Time Spent	Activity
Thursday	1/2 hour	reading Tommy Jones
Weekend	Several hours for some reason	Wrote stories
Monday	15 mins	math homework + reading
Tuesday	15 mins	Read
Wednesday	15 - 30 mins Rehearsed	Read Garfield play + recorder practice

Week of ___Feb. 22 - March 1___

Spelling words - Review test 13-18 on Monday Feb. 2

Read a book

Test on oceans and continents on Thurs., March 1
(label on a map)

Please return each Thursday

Example "M-1"
Parent Information
Feedback Form

Student's Name _____

Week _____

	Monday		Tuesday		Wednesday		Thursday		Friday	
	Good	Do Over	Good	Do Over	Good	Do Over	Good	Do Over	Good	Do Over
Math										
Hand.										
Spelling										
Language										

Parent
Signs: _____ _____ _____ _____ _____

NOTE: Parental involvement and constructive feedback can speed up the
learning process. An individualized program to create awareness
and enforce expectations might look like this for the area of
"neatness."

Student's Name _____

Week _____

	Monday		Tuesday		Wednesday		Thursday		Friday	
	Good	Do Over	Good	Do Over	Good	Do Over	Good	Do Over	Good	Do Over
Math										
Hand.										
Spelling										
Language										

Parent
Signs: _____ _____ _____ _____ _____

NOTE: Parental involvement and constructive feedback can speed up the
learning process. An individualized program to create awareness
and enforce expectations might look like this for the area of
"neatness."

Student's Name _____

Week _____

	Monday		Tuesday		Wednesday		Thursday		Friday	
	Good	Do Over	Good	Do Over	Good	Do Over	Good	Do Over	Good	Do Over
Math	☺				☺		☺			
Hand.		☹ We did it over in class	*Richard*	*forgot*	none		☺ worked together			
Spelling		Do over in cursive			none					
Language	No written assignment				ok		☺			

Parent Signs: _*djm*_____ _*djm*_____ _*djm*_____ _*djm*_____ _____

NOTE: Parental involvement and constructive feedback can speed up the learning process. An individualized program to create awareness and enforce expectations might look like this for the area of "neatness."

Student's Name _____

Week _____

	Monday		Tuesday		Wednesday		Thursday		Friday	
	Good	Do Over	Good	Do Over	Good	Do Over	Good	Do Over	Good	Do Over
Math	☺				☺		☺			
Hand.		☹ We did it over in class	*Richard*	*forgot*	none		☺ worked together			
Spelling		Do over in cursive			none					
Language	No written assignment				ok		☺			

Parent Signs: _*djm*_____ _*djm*_____ _*djm*_____ _*djm*_____ _____

NOTE: Parental involvement and constructive feedback can speed up the learning process. An individualized program to create awareness and enforce expectations might look like this for the area of "neatness."

Name_____ Date_____

ASSIGNMENT	HOMEWORK		RATING	TEACHER
Reading/Language Arts				
_____	Yes	No	_____	_____
_____				
Math:_____	Yes	No	_____	_____
_____				
Social Studies:_____	Yes	No	_____	_____
_____				
Science:_____	Yes	No	_____	_____
_____				

Rating: 0 - uncooperative, talking out
           1 - some participation, improvement needed
           2 - acceptable behavior
           3 - excellent, cooperative

Parent/guardian signature_____

NOTE:

A simple rating scale can do wonders for those few students who have
not gotten into the groove of getting homework done on time.
Parent/guardian accountability in terms of rewards and consequences
from home should make a considerable difference in a short time. Put
these pages in a little booklet to prevent them from getting lost. You
can look back together at conference time to see the progress and set
new goals.

Name_____

Animal Facts

1. Animal's Name

2. Animal's Covering

3. Animal's Food

4. Animal's Movement

5. Animal's Habitat

6. Other Interesting Animal Information

Book Name (Title)

Author

NOVEMBER REVIEW

Name _Jason_

Room Information

1. How many strikes have you had this quarter? _three_

2. How many learning center papers (stars) did you do? _64_

3. Who is your reading teacher? _Miss Anderson_

4. What was your percentage on the unit reading test? _80%_

5. Are you getting your work completed on time? _yes_

6. Name two of your friends: (1) _Mike K._

                             (2) _Brian R_

7. How many times have you participated in show and tell? _2 times_

   (What did you tell about?)

I told that I got a cirtifakit from the Mayor. coloring contest

8. What is your favorite subject? _Math_

9. Reading log _4_

Math _10_ Rdg

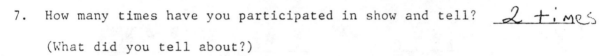

Add
$$\begin{array}{cccccc} 8 & 7 & 6 & 8 & 9 & 9 \\ +\,9 & +\,7 & +\,9 & +\,7 & +\,7 & +\,9 \\ \hline 17 & 14 & 15 & 15 & 16 & 18 \end{array}$$

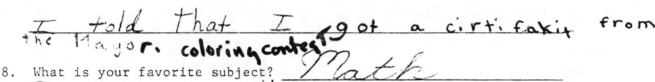

Subtract
$$\begin{array}{cccccc} 18 & 17 & 16 & 15 & 14 & 15 \\ -\,9 & -\,8 & -\,9 & -\,6 & -\,7 & -\,9 \\ \hline 9 & 9 & 7 & 9 & 7 & 6 \end{array}$$

Signs $<, >, =$

    25 $>$ 19   62 $<$ 71   852 $>$ 849

Roman Numerals

      XIX = _19_   14 = _XIV_

43

November Review
Page 2

Name *Jason*

Add or subtract

$$\begin{array}{r} ^{+1}274 \\ +\ 593 \\ \hline 867 \end{array}$$

$$\begin{array}{r} 35 \\ +\ 27 \\ \hline 52 \end{array}$$

$$\begin{array}{r} 9\overset{7\ 12}{8\,2} \\ -\ 873 \\ \hline 109 \end{array}$$

$$\begin{array}{r} \overset{3\,10}{4\,0}9 \\ -\ 120 \\ \hline 289 \end{array}$$

$$\begin{array}{r} 596 \\ +\ 237 \\ \hline 833 \end{array}$$

$$\begin{array}{r} 800 \\ -\ 122 \\ \hline 673 \end{array}$$

$$\begin{array}{r} 4\overset{0\ 17}{1\,7} \\ -\ 308 \\ \hline 109 \end{array}$$

$$\begin{array}{r} ^{+1}388 \\ +\ 92 \\ \hline 480 \end{array}$$

Round   72¢ → *70¢*   342 → *300*

Spelling

Using your green spelling card, record both the pretest and final test
for units 2, 4, 6, and 7.

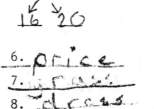

20 ↙² ↓ 20   15 ↙⁴ ↓ 20   16 ↙⁶ ↓ 20   ↙⁷ ↓

1. dime
2. night
3. spell
4. pond
5. star

6. price
7. rain
8. dress
9. rock
10. sweet

Handwriting

Make these letters in cursive: b,   a,   m,   r,   t,   h,   and   p   2X

b b a a m m

t t t t h h p p

44

November Review
Page 3

Name *Jason*

Language

1. dr jones said you have drank to much soda

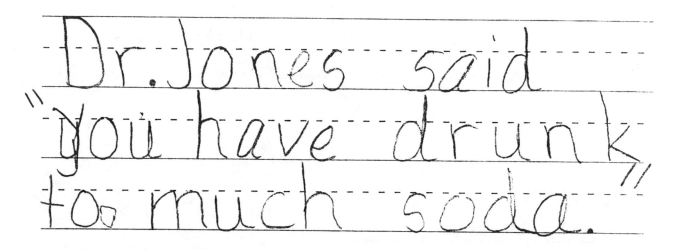

Dr.Jones said
"you have drunk
to much soda."

2. i will shares the red balloon, a book, with bill and he

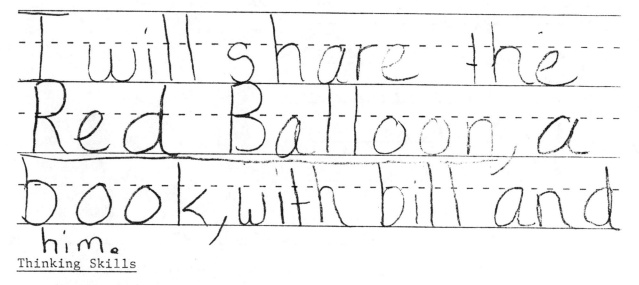

I will share the
Red Balloon, a
book, with bill and
him.

Thinking Skills

Name two thinking skills. Give examples.

1. Classifying We saw what we had on
   our finger

2. Inferences — What made it
   — what it did.

45

November Review
Page 4

P1C

Name ___Jason___

Name the Directions

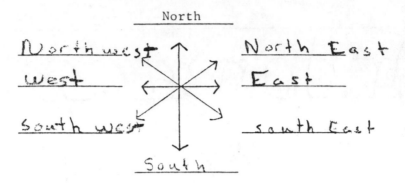

North

Northwest   North East
West   East
South west   south East

South

Name the seven continents:

1. North America
2. South America
3. Europe
4. Aisa
5. Australia
6. Antarctica
7. Africa

What hemisphere do we live in? ___Northern___

Name the states: Use page 239 (Look at the map on the back)

1. Minnesota
2. Illnois
3. Arkansas
4. Flordia
5. Maine
6. Washington
7. California
8. Wisconsin

9. Colorado
10. New York

46

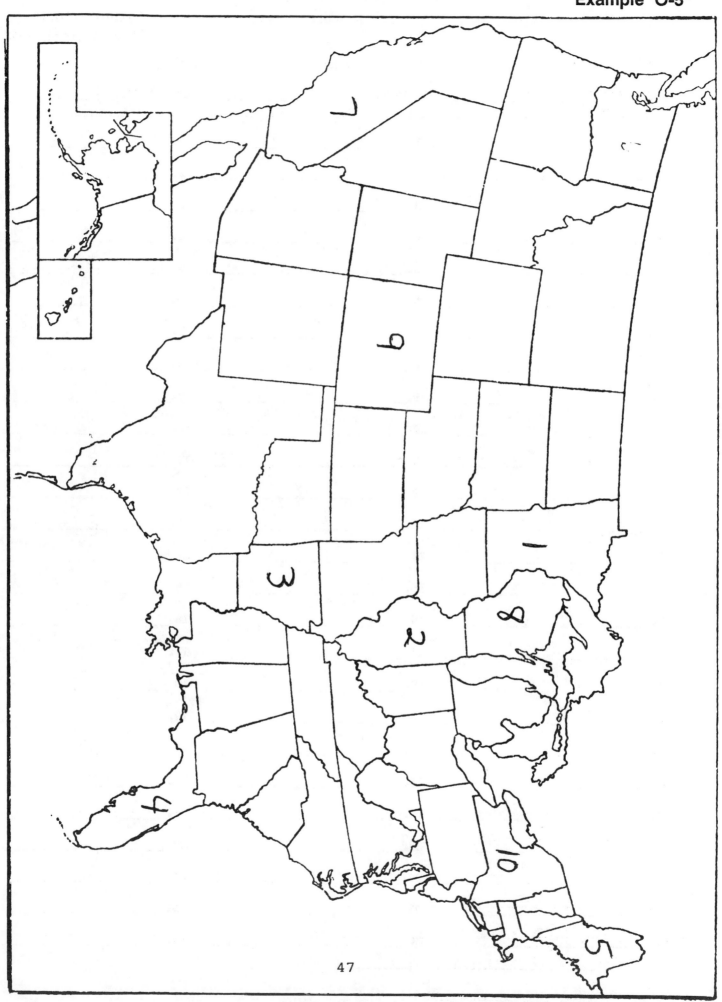

GRADE_____ Date_____

ASSIGNMENT:_____
_____

1._____
2._____
3._____
4._____
5._____
6._____
7._____
8._____
9._____
10._____
11._____
12._____
13._____
14._____
15._____
16._____
17._____
18._____
19._____
20._____
21._____
22._____
23._____
24._____
25._____
26._____

GRADE_____ Date_____

ASSIGNMENT:_____
_____

1._____
2._____
3._____
4._____
5._____
6._____
7._____
8._____
9._____
10._____
11._____
12._____
13._____
14._____
15._____
16._____
17._____
18._____
19._____
20._____
21._____
22._____
23._____
24._____
25._____
26._____

GRADE_____ Date_____

ASSIGNMENT:_____
_____

1._____
2._____
3._____
4._____
5._____
6._____
7._____
8._____
9._____
10._____
11._____
12._____
13._____
14._____
15._____
16._____
17._____
18._____
19._____
20._____
21._____
22._____
23._____
24._____
25._____
26._____

*A reminder
to parents*

Dear _____,

Don't forget! This is important!

_____

_____

_____

_____   _____
                                             date

- -

*A reminder
to parents*

Dear _____,

Don't forget! This is important!

_____

_____

_____

_____   _____
                                             date

- -

Date

Assignments completed:

Assignments to complete:

Comments:

Parent Signature

Date

Assignments completed:

Assignments to complete:

Comments:

Parent Signature

Chapter III - Papers and Files

INTRODUCTION

The paper shuffle is a fact of teaching. Included in this chapter are ways teachers have found to help minimize the overload.

Each subject area has some type of written expression which produces paper work for the teacher to deal with. How you deal with the management of these papers will dictate the amount of time and effort expended.

In this chapter, teachers suggest many ways they respond to this work in an efficient manner.

Regarding papers: "Touch me once -- ok; touch me twice, look hard; touch me three times -- time to go!"

Kathy Freeberg
Grade 5/6 teacher

NOTES:

"*The man who removes a mountain begins by carrying away small stones.*"

--Chinese proverb

COLOR CODE AM/PM

Label AM or PM papers to separate Kindergarten class papers. Color code them if you teach different groups of children throughout the day. It makes them easy to separate and funnel to the proper homeroom teacher.

INDIVIDUAL STUDENT FOLDERS

Have individual student folders for passing papers in and back. Students put papers in their folder throughout the day and are collected just once as they leave at the end of the day. The papers are then looked at and passed back the next morning to be looked at during opening exercises.

GROUPING PAPERS

When papers really pile up, streamline things by quickly separating them out into three groups: **"Have tos,"** **"Shoulds,"** and **"Throw aways."** Two smaller piles look less formidable than one larger one.

NOTES:

"Think ahead -- plan ahead -- be one step ahead to prevent or save problems."

Karen Heimer
Grade 1 teacher

PAPERWORK NOT AS DISCIPLINE

Do not assign paperwork as discipline. You want students to have pride in their work and a positive outlook toward learning. This will save you time in not having to handle needless papers or to follow up on it.

ASSIGN STUDENT A NUMBER

Assign each student a number corresponding to an alphabetized list. Have each student automatically include this number in the upper left hand corner of their papers. It is quick and easy to put them in order. Let a student do it. Then have the student put a slip of paper on top with the numbers that are missing for easy follow up.

MATH PACKETS

Assign math by chapter packets. Students are on independent progress. Instruct by small groups. Students correct their own work daily. Chapter tests are given and corrected by the teacher. Packets are sent home for parental review when finished.

COLOR CODE GRADE LEVEL

If you teach more than one grade or are in a combination classroom, color code papers for quick identification with a marker, piece of colored construction paper, sticky, or color-coded "In Basket."

PAPERS DUE

Set up assigned spaces on a bulletin board with names on colored construction paper. Special assignments are posted over their name. The colored paper makes a nice border around each paper, and it is easy to see whose paper is still due. It is a subtle motivator to not be the blank one.

PASSING PAPERS FORWARD

If your student desks are in rows, pass papers forward, putting yours on top. The front desk people pass them across from left to right putting their row's stack on top. The last person takes the stack to the teacher's "In Basket." No one has to get out of his/her seat except the last student. The front row person also is responsible for arranging the papers and checking for names. This makes it a cinch for handing papers back, as they are already in the correct order.

HAND-IN FOLDER

Make a hand-in folder for each row or group of students. They put their assignment in the folder and check off or sign their name in the appropriate square. When you collect the row's folder, you can immediately see who's paper is not there and assign make-up time as appropriate.

(Papers)

STUDENTS'
MONTHLY
BOOKLETS

Save all the students' papers by subject area. Make covers and staple all of them together as a booklet to send home every month or so. Art and pride are fostered at the same time.

RESPECT
PRIVACY

Fold papers back so that grades can't be seen by students who are passing back papers. This saves face for some and models respect for privacy.

END-OF-YEAR
SCRAPBOOKS

Set up creative writing folders. Staple a record sheet inside one cover and a skills-target sheet inside the other cover. Check record keeping and collect the papers each quarter. They make excellent additions to end-of-year scrapbooks.

NUMBERS VS
LABELING

Number baskets for turning in assignments, and then key the same item by number on the chalkboard next to the specific assignment.

EXTRA COPIES Always run off a few extra copies of things due to mistakes, reteaching, or lost papers. This, alone, will save you hours of extra footsteps and anxiety.

COLOR CODE BY SUBJECT Run off worksheets on a certain color for each subject. If only white paper is available, simply mark the edges with a colored magic marker for quick identification.

SCRATCH PADS Recycled paper is often made into small scratch pads with rubber glue binding. Have one of these for each student. They record answers only on these pads. The savings are not only in paper, but in correcting time. You can easily line up eight of these smaller answer sheets on your desk when correcting or recording. You can dub them **"Think Pads."**

CODE MASTER COPY Put a key, such as a red circle, in the top corner of original copies to be reproduced, so you do not use, give, or throw away the master copy.

COPIES FOR THE YEAR Sort out and run copies of everything you can think of needing. Have a good filing system for quick recall. This saves lots of time during the year and is a nice feeling when the copy machine is broken. Bind the packets together with masking tape on 4 sides. Paper clips are too bulky.

TEAMING CUTS WORK Team with another teacher or more to run off papers in common. Order the needed number of extra copies for all teachers. This also works well for ordering films and other equipment.

STORAGE BOX Are student desks too stuffed? Try collecting spelling notebooks and having them put in a storage box on the window sill. Students put their names in large print and custom design them for quick identification. They don't get so dog-eared. It works for other notebooks and materials also. For instance, label and collect all scissors and glue bottles.

STUDENTS PICKUP PAPERS
Don't collate booklets yourself. Simply put out the pages in piles. Have students file by in a line picking up the bottom page first, and ending up with the top page on top. Staple them at the end of the line. This assembly line arrangement can save you hours and only takes few minutes of the students' time.

GALLON CANS
Make student **mailboxes** to ease the handing out of papers. Students can play mailperson. Gallon cans laid on their side work well, as do half gallon milk cartons with the tops removed.

COLOR CODE
Color code student **mailboxes** to indicate those having an older brother or sister in the same school. Do not give them bulletins from the office, as it is just a waste of paper to send repetitive papers to the same parent/guardian.

SHOE BOXES
Have student **mailboxes**. Plastic shoebox sets, made for closets, work well. Students may take handbacks home anytime, all but all boxes must be cleaned out on Friday.

STUDENT FRIEND
Put names of absentees on papers as the class receives them. Have a student friend keep track of the assignments and explain them upon their return.

WASH PAN TUBS
Plastic wash pan tubs make excellent places to keep bulky folders and workbooks. They are just the right depth. They are also useful in handing out science or art materials to groups.

"NO TALKING" RULE
Teach the routine of **NO TALKING** while papers are being collected or handed back. It takes too long to get the group back to order. Instead you can use the time to talk, give directions, ask a few questions, or whatever.

WORKBOOKS OPEN
Collect workbooks open to the correct page and in the same order as your grade book is numbered. You don't have to locate the pages and recording is made easier alphabetically.

COLLECT BY ASSIGNED NUMBER

Assign a number to each student to be written beside each student's name. Collect papers by successive numbers for ease of recording in the grade book.

GOOD HEADINGS

It is not too much to expect a good heading with a name on homework! Teach the routine the first day of school and tell them that after the first week there will be **NO** more reminders! Any paper without a name will have to be redone. A few dramatic throw aways all but cures the problem for the rest of the year.

QUICK CHECK NO NAMES

When you have a number of papers missing and/or no names on them, do a **"quick check."** Ask all students to raise their hands or stand up. Quickly call off the students' names on the papers you have. Students lower their hands or sit down when their name is called. Students left have a paper due.

PENALTY NO NAME

If a name is not on the paper turned in for cooperative group work, the group loses a point. This promotes proofreading for themselves and others.

STUDENT(S) STAPLE PAPERS

Anytime students turn in more than one paper at a time, they should be taught the routine of having to staple them first. This saves time correcting, recording, sorting, and handing papers back.

BALANCE WORKLOAD

Try to balance out work loads over the week so all papers are not required to be turned in on one particular day. You won't find your correcting load as unmanageable if you space it out.

STUDY FOLDER

Keep pretests, chapter tests, and quizzes in student folder to be used for review prior to an end-of-level or unit test. Have a partner study time when they ask each other questions from their **"study folders."** Encourage them to review the folders periodically at home.

PAPER CLIP PAPERS

Paper clip groups of papers as soon as you collect them. Label the stack by topic, level, etc. and put them in the correct "In Basket." This will save you valuable time by not having to sort and shuffle them again later.

PAPERS FACE UP

Stress the importance of collecting and stacking papers all face up with the names at the top. This eliminates a lot of needless shuffling before you start to correct or go over them.

PRE-SORT PAPERS

Have the students help you sort incoming papers before you touch them. Set up a number of "In Baskets" for several different things instead of just having one, such as subject areas, notes for the teacher, office mail such as lunch bills, etc..

TEAR OUT WORKBOOK PAGES

Tear out workbook pages before collecting so that you don't have to handle the bulk of all those notebooks. Be sure their names are on them first.

FORM NOTE

Send home a **"form note"** to parents to cover a variety of situations. After parents reply, staple it to the student's folder for further discussion during conferences. The advantage is not having to make out individualized notes when one form can cover so many in a faster manner.
(See example "A",p.71)

HANDLE PAPERS ONCE

Try not to handle papers more than once. Do not sort out into mailboxes. Send papers home as soon as they are completed. You may even want to take down grades orally into your grade book.

SPECIAL PLACE

Put an extra student desk in an accessible spot for papers to be handed out. Students can put papers here that they do not want to lose in their desks. You can put newsletters, parent folders, corrected papers, bulletins, etc. there.
Hand everything out at the end of the day or once a week.

STUDENT VOLUNTEERS

Have a student volunteer to pick up and hand out papers during times the students are out of the room: before school, after school, lunchtime, or at break time.

STUDENT HELP

Students who finish their work early get to hand papers back during the time other students are finishing their work. This is an efficient use of time, and they get to know their classmates better, as well as, having to read their names.

"HAND OUT" AREA

Have a "Hand Out" area. Place papers to be handed back in this area. Student helpers or volunteers hand them out at an appropriate time.

BEFORE AND AFTER	If you have a number of papers per student for the day, staple them together in the correct order. You won't have to resort them all out. Collect them in order or all at one time.
STUDENT INTEREST	If a student expresses an interest in taking a certain paper home, send it home that same day for immediate reinforcement. Attach a personal note if you have time to emphasize its specialness. It is a "teachable moment."
"PASS BACK" TUB	Keep all papers in a **"Pass Back" tub**. Send them all home at one time each week, along with newsletters and bulletins. They won't get lost as easy and parents will be expecting them.
PARENT FOLDER	Parent folders that are sent home on a weekly basis can be made by stapling the two vertical edges together and gluing a cover sheet on the outside. The cover sheet should have a place for the parent to sign and date, along with an area for comments. If you run out of room for signatures, simply glue another cover sheet on top of the old one. Students may decorate the blank side as an art project or in their free time. Parents expect these each Thursday evening, sign and date the folder, and return it the very next day. Passing out papers once a week and having an area to keep "passbacks" makes for less papers lost and less daily time for passing them out. **(See examples "B" and "C", pp. 72, 73)**
PAPER SAVING	Keep all paper to make sure it is used on both sides. It models environmental awareness and saves on the school's paper budget. Back sides can be reused for spelling tests, scratch paper, other assignments, etc.
JOB LIST	Keep lists of what has to be done. Prioritize them and cross off completed items. Jotting them down means you don't have to keep remembering them, and prevents you from forgetting them. It is a good way to set goals for yourself.

NOTES:

"Consider the postage stamp: It's usefulness

consists in the ability to stick to one thing 'till it

gets done."

Josh Billings

**LETTER
SOUNDS**

Develop a "sound" file for all letters A-Z. Collect pictures, stories, songs, poems, art work, worksheets, etc. for each letter. Keep adding to your collection over the years and you have a nice selection to use.

NUMBERS

Assign each student a number. Use these to collect papers. You can teach them to sequence. They can line up by their numbers. Variations include lining up by 2's, 5's, 10's, counting forward and backward, odd and even numbers, answers to addition and subtraction facts, etc. Also, establish student files by their numbers verus names. These files can be used year after year.

"Wishing consumes as much energy as planning."

unknown

NOTES:

"About the only thing that comes to us without any effort is old age."

unknown

POCKET FOLDER Have a pocket folder for each student attached on the side of their desk. All their papers go into it throughout the day. Their names are on the outside, so you know whose folders they are. Papers are already separated out for that particular student, and they can work on them during the day. Collect at night. Any missing papers are listed by names on the chalkboard for make up the next day during recess.

FILING BASKET Have a box or basket marked "For Filing." All corrected papers and passbacks are put in this box or basket. Assigned students, then file corrected papers into the other students' individual files, mailboxes, folders, or wherever.

"Touch things only once; take care of it then, when touched."

Gwen Stanich

NOTES:

"The disciplined person is the one who does <u>what</u> needs to be done <u>when</u> it needs to be done."

Zig Ziglar

STARTING FILES
New teachers, especially, need to start developing file folders for everything immediately. It will be invaluable for saving time the second year. It is easy to let this area slip, but you'll find yourself right back in the same hurried, unorganized pattern the next year if you don't make files for each unit, theme, reading group, art project, etc.

PERIODIC FILING
Save time filing. Papers which are to be filed, but have no real time line, should be accumulated for a period of time and then all filed at once. Have a special place for these lower priority items.

PAPER BOX FILES
File things in the regular sized paper boxes that reams of paper come in. The office probably has just thrown them away in the past. They are easy to stack and need only to be labeled on one end.

WALLPAPER BOXES
Cover the cardboard boxes that reams of paper come in with wallpaper. These make great extra filing drawers and may be stacked with the subject labeled on the front.

BOX FILES
Store most things in the same size boxes. This allows for easier stacking. Write the contents on the end so it can be seen easily. This is a lifesaver if you move to different buildings, or rooms, throughout your career.

3-RING BINDERS
Use hard cover 3-ring binders for filing. Invest in a 3-hole punch, preferably the large size holes, because they do not tear out easily. They are easy to store and can be rearranged easily.

NEW IDEAS
Start a folder labeled: **"New Ideas."** Jot down that brainstorm before you forget it and put it in the folder. Sort out and file them for use next year when your schedule permits.

START OF THE YEAR
Start a folder called: **"Beginning of the School Year."** Put those "special" ideas, master sheets, and "musts" in here so you will have more time to do the unexpected. Add to it for next year as you think of things you want to do that first week. It acts much like an airplane pilot's check list.

END-OF-YEAR	Develop a folder called **"End-of-Year Activities and Duties."** Put those "special" ideas, master sheets, and "musts" in here so you won't forget them. Again, it acts as your checklist so nothing is forgotten. Add to it as the year goes on if you think of other ideas.

MASTER COPY	Put master copies on the bottom of the pile. When you get close to running out, just take the bottom sheet off and run off more. You won't have to hunt up the master if you keep it right with the pack, and file them together.

FILING AWAY	Put all things away when finished with them. You will save time looking for them, and they won't get in the way when you're using others. It's easier to file as you go, than to let it build up to an unmanageable, unsightly situation.

FILE BY SUBJECT	File by subject area all in one drawer. Put everything pertaining to that subject in that drawer, including teacher text, worksheets, tests, transparencies, pictures, etc.

STENCIL LETTERS	When filing your letter stencils, trace one of them on the outside of the file. It will give you the size and type of letter at a second's glance. It saves time looking into each folder each time. Zip lock bags work great.

WORKSHEETS	File worksheets in folders, gluing a sample copy on the outside of the folder. It will save you lots of time looking and rearranging worksheets, if you only have to look at the front of the folder rather than digging through piles that are hard to see.

EACH DAY OF THE WEEK	Label file dividers for each day of the week and behind each put a division for each subject. File one week's worth of work at a time so it is at your fingertips when needed.

FILING UNITS	Organize your reading file by units. Include worksheets, overheads, vocabulary, sight words, decoding vocabulary, spelling, creative writing, films, art projects, related music, etc. for each unit.

MONTHS/ SUBJECT AREA Establish folders by the month and subject areas. Color code subject areas for easy reference regardless of the month. Any time you see something you like, cut it out or copy it and drop it into one of the appropriate files for next time. You won't lose the idea if you act on it immediately.

YOUR BASKET Have one basket marked "**Stuff for   (your name) **." Any notes from student or parent go here. You can deal with them all at one time at your convenience versus reading each one whenever the student brings it to you.

3 X 5 CARD Keep individual student records on 3 x 5 note cards punched on a key ring. It is easy to make, alphabetical order makes it easy to use, and it doesn't take up much space. It is a natural for parent/teacher/student conferences.

BULLETINS Make a file for all school bulletins going home to parents. It is easier to refer to an item and/or answer a parent question if the bulletins are accessible.

NOTES:

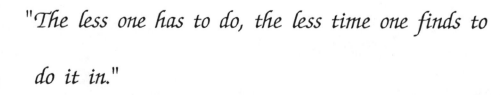

"The less one has to do, the less time one finds to do it in."

Lord Chesterfield

TO _____

DATE _____

Regarding: Behavior   Homework   Special Event

                Other:_____

TEACHER'S NOTE:

TO _____   DATE _____

PARENT(S) REPLY:

TO _____   DATE _____

==

TO _____

DATE _____

Regarding: Behavior   Homework   Special Event

                Other:_____

TEACHER'S NOTE:

TO _____   DATE _____

PARENT(S) REPLY:

TO _____   DATE _____

Folwell Elementary School

603 S.W. 15th Avenue   Rochester, Minnesota 55902   507-281-6073

Dear Parent:

As a weekly reporting tool this envelope will be sent home
each Thursday listed below. It will contain all communications
from school and show you current work done by your child.

Please review and remove all materials. Place any papers with
SAVE into your <u>Total Child District Folder</u> for future reference
and as your progress record.

Please SIGN this sheet at the appropriate date each week. RETURN
the EMPTY envelope each Friday.

Feel free to call if you have any questions. Open communications
is our goal.

Sincerely,

Mrs. Davis
Mrs. Kehoe
Mrs. Ostby

Sign and return:

*November 25:-----------------------	March 3:------------------------
December 3:-----------------------	March 10:------------------------
December 10:-----------------------	March 17:------------------------
December 17:-----------------------	March 24:------------------------
*December 23:-----------------------	March 31:------------------------
January 7:-----------------------	April 7:------------------------
January 14:-----------------------	April 14:------------------------
January 21:-----------------------	April 21:------------------------
January 28:-----------------------	April 28:------------------------
February 4:-----------------------	May 5:------------------------
February 11:-----------------------	May 12:------------------------
February 18:-----------------------	May 19:------------------------
February 25:-----------------------	May 24:------------------------
	June 2:------------------------

*Denotes Wednesday due to holiday. Return the next day school is in
session.

An Affirmative Action/Equal Opportunity Employer

72

Dear Parents,

Please plan a time for you and your child to go through the Progress Folder. Remember to return all sheets with **"save"** on them. I would appreciate it if you would write any comments, ideas or questions on the bottom of this sheet, sign and return it to me.

Thanks,

_____
Teacher's Name

Comments:

_____

_____

_____

_____
Parent Signature

Dear Parents,

Please plan a time for you and your child to go through the Progress Folder. Remember to return all sheets with **"save"** on them. I would appreciate it if you would write any comments, ideas or questions on the bottom of this sheet, sign and return it to me.

Thanks,

_____
Teacher's Name

Comments:

_____

_____

_____

_____
Parent Signature

"*Faced with having to change our views or prove*

that there is no need to so do, most of us get busy

on the proof."

--John Kenneth Galbraith,
quoted by Marilyn Ferguson in The Aquarian
Conspiracy (Jeremy P. Tarcher)

Chapter IV - Student Absences

INTRODUCTION

The methods suggested in this chapter address student absences for one period, a day or longer.

The methods you use will dictate the amount of time expended. Suggestions from teachers in this chapter will offer you ideas on how to make students more responsible for dealing with this problem.

Do you require everything to be made up? Have you considered alternate assignments based on educational needs and requirements?

NOTES:

"*Good ideas are not adopted automatically. They must be driven into practice with courageous impatience.*"

--*Adm. Hyman G. Rickow*

SET OF PAPERS

Make a set of papers for each student before the day starts. Hand out all papers for the day at one time. Simply set aside a set for any absent student. It saves time passing out papers for each class, and makes for easy assigning of make-up work.

ASSIGNMENT SHEETS

Run off a number of blank assignment sheets. A designated student keeps track of assignments throughout the day. An extra set of work papers and materials is also kept with it. At the end of the day it is either sent home with a close neighbor, kept for a parent to pick up, or for the student when he/she comes back the next day.
(See examples "A" and "B", pp. 83-84)

ENVELOPES

Establish an **"Absent Student(s) Envelope."** Hang this up in the room to put missed assignments and "To do" papers in. Returning students go to this area upon their return to find make-up work.

TELEPHONE CALL

Don't rule out a quick call home to the parent to give an update on activities missed. It is good PR and is quick.

PARTNER

Assign partners for the entire year. They have the responsibility to write down assignments missed, to gather extra worksheets and materials needed, and to write get well and/or welcome back notes to the absentee. This takes the burden off the teacher and teaches responsibility to the students. This works great when students are absent from the room for short periods of time.

NOTES:

"PATIENCE is the ability to let your light shine

after your fuse has blown."

--Quoted by Bob Levey in Washington Post

TAKING WORK HOME

Make a list of who is to take "make-up" work home for each student, who may become absent. It may be a brother or sister from school, a neighbor, classmate, parent, or friend. Don't forget to get details such as name, room number, grade, address, telephone number, classroom teacher, etc.

GET-WELL CARD

If a student is sick for more than one day, pass out a form **"get-well"** card for all to sign. The parent or a good friend delivers the make-up work along with the card. You might even assign someone to give the absent student a call of encouragement and remembrance in the evening.

JOURNAL

For students traveling for a week or more outside of school, assign a special journal. They keep a daily log of their trip as a language arts activity. It is too hard to expect them to make up all the material covered in school. If you have enough advance warning, tests can be taken in advance of their leaving or given by the parents during the trip.

ROTATING CLASSES

If a child sees more than one teacher, develop a form for another student to carry to each of the teachers in order to gather the assignments missed by a classmate.

NOTES:

"There are no hopeless situations, only people

who have lost hope."

Anonymous

BLANK FORM   Make up a blank form with a cute get-well wish on it. Run off copies and either you or a student keeps a running list of assignments throughout the day. Make a quick copy on the duplicator machine so that you have a list to double check with. (Just in case the student's copy gets misplaced.) **(See example "C", p. 85)**

PAPER CLIPS   Establish a recipe box with 3 x 5 cards for each student. Not only is this used as record keeping for conferences, but when a student is absent, put a paper clip on that card to indicate work needs to be made up. Remove the clip when the student has finished the work. Different colored paper clips can be used to code different subject areas or needs.

COOPERATIVE GROUPS   Assign cooperative groups or a **"buddy"** to each student. When the student returns they look in a special folder to find their assignments, worksheets, materials, etc. Any questions can also be answered by the other student(s). It is also helpful, to have the student taking the assignments down, to include their home telephone number in case there is a question the next evening. This also works when students are gone for short periods of time during the day like going to special area teachers, lavatory, and office calls.

NOTES:

"*A wise man will make more opportunities than he finds.*"

--*Frances Bacon*

ASSIGNMENTS FOR THE WEEK OF _____

NAME OF STUDENT _____

	MONDAY	TUESDAY	WEDNESDAY	THURSDAY	FRIDAY
MATH					
ENGLISH					
READING					
SCIENCE					
SOCIAL STUDIES					
SPELLING					
NOTES					

Absent Student:	Date:
Student Name:	Teacher:
Reading	Math
Spelling	Writing
Science	Health
Social Studies	English
Positive Action	Other

84

Name_____

Dates_____

"You Were Missed"

Subject	Assignment	✔ When Complete ✔

If you have any questions, check with a peer before you ask me.

Name_____

Dates_____

"We Missed You"

Subject	Assignment	✔ When Complete ✔

If you have any questions, check with a peer before you ask me.

Chapter V - Correcting Papers

INTRODUCTION

Correcting papers is a necessity in teaching that needs to be addressed in a productive manner.

Papers can be assessed in many different ways depending upon the subject, type of work, and individual students. The more informed you are about each student, the better you are at being able to deal with individual needs. Your diagnosing and prescribing will match better the individual student needs.

We hope some of your problems will be solved by these proven, effective ways of correcting papers.

"Why is there never enough time to do things right, but always enough time to do it over?"

Gwen Stanich

NOTES:

"Be dissatisfied enough to improve, but satisfied enough to be happy."

--J. Harold Smith

OLD DATE   Teach the routine of putting the date on their headings. If the date is too old, do not bother correcting them and vow to do better in the future.

#	NAME	SUBJECT	DATE

COMMENT   Have students keep their papers for a half day or whole day. Staple them all together as a packet to be reviewed by the teacher. A comment of **"top day," "so-so day,"** or **"fair day"** can be added for the parent to get an idea of comparable progress.

SAME ORDER   **Collect** papers in the same order as they appear in your grade book. This is a big time-saver. **Record** grades at the same time you correct them.

TOP STUDENT HELPER   When doing independent practice in math assign a top student to three other students. When the top student is finished, it is his/her responsibility is to check the answers of the other three.

SELF-CORRECTION   Set up a **"Self-Correcting"** station near your desk. Pupils cannot bring any pencil with them, but can use the special pen provided along with the answer sheet. Laminate keys to be used year-to-year.

START EARLY   Usually certain students finish their work first, so you can correct their papers right away while the others are still working. Don't wait until everyone is finished to start correcting.

HANDLE ONCE   Try to handle papers only once. Correct, grade, and record all at once. Students come with papers to the teachers when completed. Independent, positive choices of activities is promoted. Immediate, specific feedback is allowed. Questions for clarification are easily answered. After recorrections, the papers are put into their individual student folders by themselves.

SHORT TIME PERIODS — Correct a little bit each short time period you have free throughout the day. Sponging up these free minutes will result in smaller amounts of paper work, which pile up all day long.

CHECK TOP STUDENTS — Always check a few top students' papers first. If they are having trouble, throw away all the papers, and reteach the lesson to the entire class. Don't waste time correcting all those problem papers.

LOTS OF ERRORS — If you start to see lots of errors on a paper, stop correcting and mark **"see me"** on the top. It saves correcting time and is a jumping-off place for a little one-on-one reteaching.

ONE PAPER PER GROUP — Check one paper per group of four students and hand that paper back. The rest of the group can correct their own papers from that one. This works well when the answers are objective in nature.

ONE-TO-ONE — It is advantageous to correct creative writing one-on-one. Reading and discussing the story structure together allows clearer communication, than that provided by the teacher's written feedback.

NEXT UP — When correcting with a student at the desk one-on one, have each successive student go tell the next one to come up to the desk. It eliminates disrupting independent workers by calling out names.

STUDENT READING — Schedule times to hear students read their creative writing to you. You have the advantage of immediate questioning so that you don't have to guess what the student was trying to say or write.

POSITIVE ANSWERS — Never use **RED** correcting pens. It gives many people a negative feeling. Instead, score positive answers with some other color. + _6_ **out of** _10_ .

NUMBER CORRECT — Always count the number **"correct"** and use that as a grade on the student's paper. Emphasis on the positive helps to build self-esteem.

STUDENT HELP
A student helper from the class or a higher grade can be utilized to correct extra credit worksheets in math, etc. Choose a dependable student you have taught in the past.

VOLUNTEER
Contact your volunteers in education. Parents are a rich resource for timely duties such as correcting and recording weekly spelling tests.

MOVE THE AMOUNT
Assign just the odd numbered problems or questions. This gives you half the amount to correct, yet still gives you a sampling of each concept. The even numbered ones are held in reserve for drill, extra practice, or reteaching.

WRITTEN COMMENTS
Let the students correct most of their own papers and use the time you save to make meaningful, written comments on the papers. They learn by going over the material again, too.

SELF-CORRECTION
Have students correct all their own work and recheck the papers. It is very important for students to see their own mistakes and how they made them. Understanding and a feeling of success and improvement are motivational. Perhaps set a qualification of any paper with over "X number" of mistakes must be re-corrected and handed in. Don't worry about perfection, but about the process of learning before moving on to the mastery level.

STUDENT CIRCLE
Have students circle wrong answers in colored pencil, then they can go back and correct after they go over it. The next corrections can be made in yet another color.

PROOFREAD AHEAD
Before a creative writing is handed in to you, have the writer proofread it and one other student proofread it. This eliminates the easy mistakes and creates an audience for the literature. Have the proofreader sign off on the back of the paper for accountability.

CIRCLE TWO BEST
In handwriting, have the students circle their best two examples of each item. Then you have to look at only those circles instead of everything on the paper.

ADD INTEREST
To add interest to correcting papers in class, pass around an old **smoke alarm**. As each answer is read by someone else, the alarm is passed to someone else. If the person with the alarm does not agree with the answer read, they push the button. This **"alarms"** the class and the answer is discussed before going on.

"CORRECTING" PARTNER	Assign a **"Correcting Partner"** to be used for long periods of time, or the whole year. The "Partner" puts his/her name in the front of the other student's workbook, so the teacher knows who is doing the correcting. The spin-offs are reading, learning, and communication skills. Again, it is saving time for more important tasks such as diagnosing and prescribing.
SMALL GROUP	Assign a small group, perhaps those that finished an assignment first, to correct all papers of the class in a specific subject area. Set up a **"correcting table."**
TWO-PART PAPERS	Anytime you have two pages of papers to correct, do just one at a time. This eliminates paper shuffle noise and focuses attention on one part at a time.
LAMINATE ANSWER SHEETS	If you use the same answer sheet year after year, or if lots of students use it, increase its durability by laminating it, or simply putting clear contact paper on both sides of it.
RECORD PAPERS FOR CORRECTION	Use the front of the student's workbook to record page numbers that must be recorrected. The page numbers are crossed off if satisfactorily redone. The record is never lost and can be effectively used during Parent-Teacher-Child Conferences.
"BUBBLE SHEETS"	Use **"bubble sheets"** to be machine scored by a scanner or by hand with an overlay. A magic marker in the marked circles shows which ones were missed.
ANSWERS IN COLUMNS	If answers are in columns (design your assignments this way on purpose), lay 6-10 papers side by side so just the answers are showing. Correct across the page one answer at a time. Correcting one paper at a time is inefficient.
TEST ANSWER SHEETS	Have students write their answers on an answer sheet for tests of more than one page. This makes them easier to check and the tests remain reusable.

"DIPSTICK"

Put the weaker students on top of the pile. Review their papers without grading them. This gives you direction in future lessons and acts as a **"dipstick"** to check how well you've taught the lesson.

"HOLISTIC" SCORING

Get training in **"Holistic Scoring of Creative Writings."** It is much faster and it assigns an overall score of 0-4 for the paper.

GROUPS EDITING

After a writing assignment, divide your class into four groups. Each group is in charge of editing papers for different kinds of mistakes. Papers are passed from group to group. When a student gets his own paper back, it has been proofread for errors in punctuation, spelling, capitalization, and has been read aloud. Proofreaders indicate (in pencil) on the paper where they think errors exist.

BOYS/GIRLS EACH WEEK

If your students do a particular writing assignment each week that takes you a great deal of time to correct, have the girls do it one week and the boys the following week. That way, you only have half as much work to correct each week.

"Step-by-step learning...anyone can learn anything if the steps are small enough."

Sandy Knopp

NOTES:

"Never make the same mistake once."

anonymous

STUDENT TYPEWRITTEN WORK
Using the computer or typewriter makes it easier to correct creative writing. Have the students double space everything so that inserts are easier to make.

STUDENTS CHECK WORK FIRST
Teach the students the routine of having to check two resources before you. The resources may be a dictionary, encyclopedia, library center, a peer, a parent, etc. You will have less correcting to do and more time in which to do it.

NUMBER OF ERRORS
In proofreading exercises, tell the students the number of errors they are to find in a certain text. This keeps them looking longer and fewer mistakes are handed in.

EVERY THIRD PAPER
Let students and parents know that you correct only every third paper randomly. For daily work, it cuts your work load by two-thirds, and the students are still accountable for doing their best.

STUDENTS SELECT
Correct one out of three creative writings and have them rewritten in final correct form. Perhaps have children choose their favorite out of the three to be finalized and displayed on a bulletin board or published in a booklet.

DO NOT WAIT
Don't correct papers and then ask who wasn't finished. Always check for assignments finished, first. The ones that aren't done can work on that while the rest are correcting. They have to correct their own on break time, of course.

COOPERATIVE GROUP
Have each Cooperative Learning Group focus on one particular part of an assignment and correct several papers. Group A could correct for capitalization; Group B for spelling; Group C for grammar, etc. A lot of learning is positively directed while getting the papers corrected at the same time. The teacher establishes the criteria and manipulates the results.

FEWER PAPERS
Use more cooperative group learning so that three to five students turn in one project or paper to correct. Individual accountability comes later with tests, quizzes, or assessments.

ROTATE WORK
Schedule groups on a rotation basis over a period of time. For example, if you teach several groups of math, don't meet with all of them on the same day or your paper work will stack up too quickly.

STUDY PERIOD
Schedule in a study period and use the time to correct papers. If there is a special problem, call the student up to the desk and solve it immediately.

STUDENTS READ ANSWERS
There are several advantages to having the students read the answers to the class when correcting. It takes a little more time, however, it improves reading skills, vocabulary, voice projection, and following along. It also gives the teacher time to observe students individually while they correct.

ANSWER KEY
Answer keys for many students can be done just one time if you use the chalkboard and/or overhead transparency. Everyone can see it at the same time.

CALCULATORS
Let the students use calculators for grading percentages on their own papers. You will be integrating technology and math skills with a highly motivational activity, while you save time doing it yourself.

TOTAL CLASS
Correct as a total class, all at one time. Vary by correcting someone else's paper. Use a different colored marking pen. This acts as one more review of the material and saves you having to check all those papers yourself.

RANDOM SELECTION
Correct math with a random selection of problems. Why check each and every answer? Correct a sampling of each section in class together. Students can correct their papers on their own, if they wish. It saves time, keeps students accountable, and minimizes questions by focusing on the concept rather than the specific problem.

PRE-TESTS
Students are perfectly capable of correcting their own pre-tests in spelling. Have them write the correct spelling next to the incorrect one for studying before the final spelling test.

COMPETENT STUDENTS
Have competent students correct papers on a confidential basis. However, do not let them check final assessments or tests. They enjoy the responsibility. You save time.

DIFFERENT COLOR
Students should use a different colored checking instrument than the paper was done with. "All pencils away; take out your checking pens." Only mark wrong answers or the papers start looking like star constellations.

ALL IN BEFORE CORRECTING

Don't correct a group of papers until they are **all** in. It takes too much time to relocate the key, find the correct page in the grade book, and record individual papers.

PAPER CLIP KEY PAGE(S)

Put a paper clip on all key pages needed to correct. This is especially useful with students working at many different levels. Colored paper clips could be coded to certain groups for even faster reference for students or yourself.

TWO THINGS AT ONCE

Do two things at once. Listen to sports events or hobby shows while correcting papers at home. Broaden your horizons while getting the job done at the same time.

PRE- AND FINAL TEST

Fold the spelling pre-test in half. Give the final test on the blank side. When you open up the paper you will see the key on the left and the final test to correct next to it. It will be easy for another student, an aide, a volunteer, or the student himself/herself to correct it.

SELF-CORRECTION

Give each child a red pencil to use for corrections. After a math assignment, have students put away their regular pencils and get out their red correcting pencils. Students circle in red any wrong answers as you call them out. After checking papers, students may get out their regular pencils and rework problems that were wrong. When you collect papers, use a blue pencil to mark problems (circled in red) that are still wrong.

CALCULATOR CHECK ANSWERS

If students can demonstrate the concept and know the process of math computation, let them use the calculator to check answers or to do parts of their assignments. It is a real motivator, and they get to know how to operate the machine.

CHECKING SELF-CORRECTION

Even though you may have students self-correct, always look over their corrected papers to learn the types of errors they are making. It provides focus for you in teaching the next skill, computation, process, or concept. Your future teaching and individual attention depends on studying **all** correct papers.

NOTES:

REVIEW PAPERS	Look at and review papers as students are working on them. These papers done during guided practice may not have to be corrected at all, and the students may take them home immediately.
ANSWER KEYS	Make student self-correcting answer keys for students out of 3 x 5 note cards. They are easy to store and file for years to come. Store by subject and by dates in a recipe box. Also, they could be laminated for larger use by students.
VERBAL FEEDBACK	Eliminate as many marks on papers as possible. Use a + or a -. Students already know quality, and if you work one-on-one, the verbal feedback is enough.
WRITTEN COMMENTS	Write comments on papers. Students really pay attention to these compared to scores and numbers. The personal touch gets the point across much stronger. Handwriting has more of an impact than stamps.
POST-IT STICKY	Write all corrections or messages on Post-It notes and attach to the student papers. This eliminates all the messsy scratching and marks.
RUBBER STAMP	Use rubber stamps to streamline teacher notations on papers. Students may be allowed to stamp their own papers. Rotate the stamps periodically for variety.
CHECK PRACTICE PAPERS	Mark only the papers that go home. Not every paper needs to be graded, marked, and handed back. Practice papers can be checked but not graded or recorded!
ORGANIZING PAPERS	As you correct papers, lay them out in numerical order, alphabetical order, or by instructional groups so that future filing, recording, or handing them back is facilitated.
MOTIVATION	Have students read their corrected, finished copies of creative writings to the whole class. It motivates them to have an audience, and adds incentive for correcting them well before sharing in front of peers.
THREE ERRORS	If students miss more than three examples, I check out to see where I went wrong.

NOTES:

"Running with patience is perseverance in the long run."

Anonymous

Chapter VI - Record Keeping

TEACHER PLEASE NOTE: Please be aware that many of the ideas shared by teachers can and do transcend across several grade levels. Be sure to read all grades' suggestions in order to profit from the many other excellent ideas.

INTRODUCTION

Record keeping is mandatory for diagnosing, doing reports, and conducting conferences. Data is essential to support this. Begin collecting data early; even the first week of school pays dividends.

Recording specific social, academic, emotional and physical growth and development can provide a solid basis for future use. All recordings should be dated which may provide additional information related to growth of the students and class. Pretesting is an excellent method of establishing a base line for each student. It is a valuable time-saver in planning and delivery of instruction.

NOTES:

"When you have got a thing where you want it, it is a good thing to have it where it is."

Winston Churchill

PURCHASE FORMS

Purchase a grid board for charting students' progress. Laminate it and use a grease pen. It can be reused indefinitely. Many sizes and designs can be made or purchased. **(See example "L", p. 125)**

Book title: <u>Grids & Charts Handiart For the Creative Teacher</u>, Dale Seymour Publications, P.O. Box 10888, Palo Alto, CA 94303.

CONTENTS

SELF-ASSESSMENT Students should be involved with their own assessments. Social and academic areas are easily and quickly assessed to be used by you for conferences and in the classroom. **(See examples "D" & "E", pp. 117-118)**

STUDENTS OWN CHART Have students make out their own record chart blanks and suggest their own headings. This works for permission slips for field trips, thank you notes, and other form announcements.

TEACH SELF-RECORDING Teach the students to keep their own records. Turn over as much as possible to the students. Dates and scores could be recorded in their own folders. This serves as a motivator, as immediate reinforcement, and allows them to see and know their own progress of improvement.

SELF-PROGRESS Make student record/goal sheets for them to keep track of their progress. It may be a "maze of stepping stones." Each "stone" lists the page number of each successive lesson, score, possible right. Test results are also shown. These records are an invaluable tool for conferences and must be kept in a safe place so that they are not lost. **(See example "K", p. 124)**

EXAMPLES OF WORK Do not keep grades. Instead keep carefully chosen examples of student's work in all subject areas. It is a concrete record of growth without a value given. Put them altogether at the end of the year for the student to take home. Use for parent-teacher-child conferences.

DAILY JOURNAL Record student cognitive and affective progress through a daily journal. They write each day in their logs. You just look them over once a week, and pick out things to work on, and share with parents at conference. Occasionally assign the topic, such as evaluate themselves, evaluate you as a teacher, different subject areas, etc.

INDIVIDUAL CONFERENCE FORM Develop an individual conference form to be reused. Divide into two vertical sections. On the teacher side include items you wish to bring up in the conference in chronological order, putting the open-ended "fillers" at the end. On the parent's side, put items they request by phone or written communique, goals from the previous conference, etc. Three conferences can fit on one sheet so that there is easy reference and only one sheet per student per year is needed. **(See example "A", p. 113)**

INDIVIDUAL FOLDERS

Have a folder for each child for each subject area. Keep the corrected papers for parent conferences. Items might include goal-setting sheets, end-of-unit tests, spelling progress chart, reading log for library books, creative writings, assessment tests, etc.

FLIP CARD FILE

Make a **"Flip Card File."** Start with a pocket folder. Start at the bottom and fasten successive 5 x 8 index cards to the folder. Use clear tape along the top edges of the cards so that they can be lifted up and down. Student names are placed on the last line of each card, alphabetically. Only the names show. Start a new file for each quarter. They are very handy at conference time and can include final grades, goals, discipline problems, honors, etc. The cards are easy to find and can not slip out and get all mixed up.

INDIVIDUAL ASSESSMENTS

Do individual assessments while students work independently. Individual student conferences really allow you to know the individual student. Record data of past, present, and future work and expectations.

EXTRA HELP

Save time shuffling through papers to record grades. Have students or a volunteer read them off to you as you record them in your grade book. This saves a lot of time.

RECORD SMALLER NUMBER

As you correct papers, make two piles. Put 100% ones separate from those with one or more wrong. When you record scores, put the less than 100% ones in first. Circle any absentees. By a matter of elimination, all the rest have scored 100%, so just fill in all the rest of the blanks with a *.

This also works with hot lunch count. Note the smallest number choice first, the absentees second, and fill in the largest number choice automatically.

GRID SHEET

By keeping your records on grid sheets in a three-ring binder, you can lay them out side-by-side when making out report cards. This eliminates the turning of pages back and forth all the time.

GRADE BOOK ORDER

Organize your grade book in the same order as the subjects appear on the report card. This eliminates time-consuming flipping of pages back and forth.

HIGHLIGHT ERRORS

On math papers, highlight wrong answers with a yellow highlighter. When students make corrections, they can easily locate problems that need to be corrected because they are highlighted. When papers are returned to you for rechecking, you just look at highlighted problems.

BY QUARTERS

Leave spaces in your regular grade book after each name and then label the spaces **1st Quarter**, **2nd Quarter**, etc. This will allow you an allotment and get all year's records in one place.

COLOR CODE

Color code things. For example:

Pretest	yellow
Final test	pink
Review	green
Unit I	one color
Unit II	a different color

COLOR CODE GROUPS

Color code your groupings:

Blue	"Let students go."
Green	"OK, normal progress."
Red	"Need to be monitored closely."

HIGHLIGHT RETESTS

Highlight all retests so that you can check on individuals <u>and</u> your pacing of instruction. Too many retests might signal for the need to reteach and slow down the pace a bit.

CORRECTING MATH

On math papers, circle wrong answers. After student corrects the problem, write a "K" next to it. Now it will say: "OK."

First Correction   Student's Correction and OK'ed

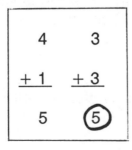 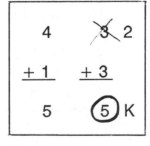

**WRITING
RECORD**

If you believe creative writing is important, start a writing folder for each student. They color the outside covers. Staple a record sheet in the back and a skills check off sheet in the front cover. Write journals, stories, poems, letters, invitations, book reports, use spelling words in stories, etc. Students may check areas of skills they think they know well and you can initial them when you are in agreement.
(See examples "G" & "H", pp. 120-121)

"Save everything."

Dan Hill

NOTES:

"Time is a circus, always packing up and moving away."

Ben Hecht

LARGER GRID	Make or purchase larger grid paper. Design your own grade book sheets. Run them on different colored paper by subject area. You will be able to find your place faster and have larger squares to write in behind each student's name. A three-ring binder works well to house them.
ENLARGE GRADE BOOK	Use the copier to enlarge grade book pages. It gives you more room to write, and they are easier to see. You won't have all those separate, more detailed plan sheets to keep track of.
SCORE/ POSSIBLE SCORE	Record grades as a plus score/possible score (6/10). Then circle the two when the paper has been corrected (6/10)
KEY SYSTEM	Make up a key system for your grade book to save time and space. Example:

> "**X**" = turned in
> "**O**" = Late
> "**⊗**" = Late and turned in
> "**a**" = absent

BLANK FORM	Spend time to make up blank forms for each subject. They are used to record a complete chapter's work. Send them home for parents to see. Copy them to review during parent-teacher-child conference. **(See example "B", p. 114)**
THREE-RING BINDER	Using a three-ring binder with blank copies of a grade book allows you to start fresh each quarter using new pages. It is easy to reorganize at any time, substitute, and add to without getting things out of order.
CARD FILE	Save time by not having to look through separate pages of your grade book and records during conference. Develop a 5 x 8 **Student Profile Card System** which lists all concepts taught and the results for the quarter. Reproduce the generic headings and sections to save time setting up the cards. Then simply fill in the blanks and you're ready. Put them into a card file or punch a hole for the snap rings. **(See example "I", p. 122)**
REPRODUCE GRID	Type your class list just once on a grid and run off as many copies as needed. Put in a three-ring binder or use on a clipboard. Students can also use it to check their names off next to the hand-in basket for assignments.

NAMES IN GRADE BOOK

Write all the names into your garde book only **ONCE**. Cut out all the rest of the parts of the pages that normally cover up the name list. This way you only have one list of names to be viewed for all the rest of the pages. Another option would be to write the list **ONCE**, run off multiple copies of the whole page, and put them in a three-ring binder. Either way, you save a lot of name writing.

VISUAL PROGRAMS CHART

Make visual math facts progress charts to record mastery. Fact test every five days. Students color in squares to show their progress in **+**, **--**, **x**, and **--**. It is a handy record to help make report cards out with.

HELP FOR GRADE BOOK

To reinforce worn grade sheets, right hand edges can be reinforced with masking tape. Adding identifying tabs also helps you find your place easier.

TEACH AS WELL AS RECORD

Teach mean, mode, and range as a math concept. Students figure their own scores and you simply record them while they practice the concept throughout the year. Integrate with calculators.

ROUND OF PERCENTAGE

Round off percentage to the nearest 10 and drop the zero. 8% becomes 90, which becomes just a **9** in your grade book. 83% equates to just an **8**. This saves space and the scores all balance out within a range of .05%.

COMPUTER RECORD
An integrated program for the computer is called **"Micro Soft Works."** It is used for grades, newsletters, etc.

APPLE PROGRAM
A computer program entitled **"Compu Grade"** (From Apple) does all the percentages for individuals and the total class.

COMPUTER AVERAGES
There is an Apple Computer program from MECC (MN Education Computer Consortium) called **"Grade Manager."** It averages grades automatically and keeps data secure, neat, and readily available.

IBM PROGRAM
IBM has a computer grading program called **"Teach the Teacher."** It averages grades for you, prints out individual scores, has word processing capabilities for personalized notes to parents or students, etc. Students can even enter their own scores.

"EASY GRADER"
Purchase a slide rule for figuring percentages. **"Easy Grader"** is made by Slide Chart, Perry Craft, L.A. CA 91324-3552; stock #5703. It also can be purchased from St. Paul Book & Stationery, P.O. Box 64410, St. Paul, MN 55164, Phone (800) 592-9522. It figures percentages for as few as eight answers or as many as 95 answers.

WORD PROCESSING
Use the computer. Word processing keeps information from year to year for easy reference. It is easy to add to or change. A printer allows quick reprinting of permission forms, unit assignments, contracts, word lists, teacher made tests, etc.

COLOR LINES
Rule your gradebook after each unit or quarter with a colored line drawn vertically. It sets a "finished" tone and makes things faster to find.

LETTER "LOOK-A-LIKES"
If you use two letters that look alike to record (such as the "M" for Mastery and "N" for Non-mastery), try circling one or the other for easier recognition: ("N").

BLANK SPACE
To help you locate more important grades in your grade book, simply leave a blank on either side of that grade. You will appreciate this when you make out report cards.

LATE WORK   A simple code to indicate late work is to **"shade"** in 1/2 of the square in your grade book. It is easy to mark over, while leaving an easy visual to see.

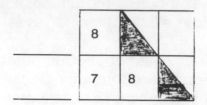

**RECORD
IN PENCIL**   Record everything in pencil. Students can redo assignments to raise their grade(s) anytime. Changes are made neatly. It is easier to erase a line when a student moves away.

**TWO-PART
RECORDING**   Record two-part assignments with the two parts of an X. "/" shows that the 1st part is done and "\" shows that the 2nd part was finished.

HIGHLIGHTS   Use a highlighter marker for every other vertical or horizontal column in your grade book. It makes it easier for your eyes to follow down and not skip into another column.

**SIZE OF
RECORD**   Record passing scores in large numerals and non-passing scores in smaller numerals. Patterns are easier to see and reteaching plans are better laid from this visual data.

9
4
8

**PRE-POST
TEST**   Impose a darker colored thin-lined marker over a lighter colored thick-lined marker to indicate pre- and post-tests completed, two-part assignments, redos, etc.

**"WEIGHTING"
RECORDS**   Use different colored ink in your record book to signify weighted items, important test scores, or below-passing grades so they stand out.

**"WEIGHTING"
FACTOR**   Record items with a **"weighting"** factor. For example:

Daily Work   X1 = score   **i.e., 6 X 1 = 6**
In-between Projects   X2 = score   **i.e., 6 X 2 = 12**
Test Work   X3 = score   **i.e., 6 X 3 = 18**

SIGNATURE STAMP

Have your name put on a **"signature stamp."** Save writing your name hundreds of times a year. It is especially useful in signing report cards and cumulative folders. A self-inking, no mess stamp of your signature can be purchased for $12.50 from GPI Printing, 510 North Prior Avenue, St. Paul, MN 55104 or check your local print shops.

FILLING OUT REPORT CARDS

Fill out report cards in the room. You can look at the child's desk and visualize the circumstances. It gives a more personal insight about the fairness and process. You will feel better not having to do them at home, too.

CLIPBOARD RECORDING

Carry a clipboard with class lists on it. Check for things such as...
1. academic work
2. behavior
3. responsibility
4. one-on-one informal guided practice
5. hand dominance
6. social interaction

This data is useful for short- and long-range planning, as well as parent conferences.

INDIVIDUAL STUDENT RECORD

Use a recipe box with 3 x 5 note cards to record various items about each student. Alphabetical dividers allow fast location of students. Record goals, health needs, conference items, tardy records, etc.

RECORD BY NUMBER

Recording by student number is much faster than looking for names. Have them put their assigned number beside their names on their papers. Also set up their personal files by number. This way you do not have to change the names each year. The numbers will always be "ready to go."

FIRST NAMES

Make your class list out alphabetically <u>by first names</u>. Being used to calling your students by their first names, makes it easier to find them without having to always recall a less-used last name.

USE OF PAPER CLIPS

Use paper clips in each child's record folder to separate papers by subject areas.

POCKET FOLDER

Use pocket folders for student papers instead of file folders. The papers do not slip out as easily. Students can tastefully decorate them.

COLOR CODING Color code your grade book for different subjects, days, groups, semesters, etc. You can find your place or retrieve information at a quick glance. It is very effective during parent-teacher-child conferences.

COLOR CODE TEAM MEMBER When teaming with other teachers, select a color for each teacher. Everything is then keyed to that color. Worksheets, grade slips, pencils, passes, notepads, etc. are easier sorted out and recognized.

POSSIBLE CORRECT Put the possible correct just one time at the top of the column! Why repeat it? 10/15 becomes just a 10. It is easier to fit into those tiny squares, too.

PROGRESS SHEETS If the district requires specific, individual progress sheets, do not record the scores in two places. Just do them one time. Don't re-record them in your grade book.

STUDENT TRANSFER SLIPS Students should be doing as much clerical work themselves as possible. If they can color in or mark their own progress charts, let them. Your time is too valuable for that. Fill in as much generic information on Student Transfer Slips as possible. Then run off several copies. It saves rewriting the same things over and over again when students transfer to another school during the year.

READING VERIFICATION FORM Using too much time checking to see if students really read their library books? Send home parent/guardian reading verification forms. A quick child's name, book's title, author, and parent's signature is all that is necessary. It also makes it easier for the child to record the book when they return to school. They just have to copy it off the form. *Remind parents of lower grades to print.
(See examples "C" and "C1", pp. 116 - 116c)

FEEDBACK FOR THE TEACHER Good data about yourself is hard to come by. If your personality can handle it, student evaluation of the teacher is usually very honest and valuable in adjusting your delivery and personality. It is a good feeling to get affirmations as to what you think you are like, also. Give it a try periodically throughout the year, or just once at the end.
(See example "F", p. 119)

Student_____

1st Conference   Date _____

Teacher	Parents

Goal -

2nd Conference   Date _____

Teacher	Parents

Goal -

3rd Conference   Date _____

Teacher	Parents

Goal -

Student _____

1st Conference   Date _Thursday, November 16_

Teacher	Parents
Extremely polite Some reversals Not enough confidence When asked (or made) to sound out words, she can do it. Good worker but could do assignments more carefully. Goal - Printing	

Needs more confidence. Work on sounding out words.

2nd Conference   Date _February 1, 1990_

Teacher	Parents
Super expression! Work on neatness — daily work Goal - Keep reading.	

3rd Conference   Date _____

Teacher	Parents
     Goal -	

113a

Math Evaluation

Name _____

Date _____

Concepts Presented	Papers Completed	Papers Missing	Percentage Score	Evaluation Indicator
				☐ Understands concepts and works with few errors
				☐ Understands concepts, but needs to reduce number of errors
				☐ Understands concepts, but percentage score reduced because of missing papers
				☐ Needs more practice with concepts presented
				☐ Needs more practice with concepts presented percentage score further reduced because of missing papers
				☐ Appropriate behavior

Teacher:

Comments:

Parent Signature

Name _____

Date _____

Math Evaluation

Concepts Presented	Papers Completed	Papers Missing	Percentage Score	Evaluation Indicator
Chapter 4 Mult. by 10's Roman Numerals Factors & products in mult. Solving for unknowns in mult. Algebra + number patterns. Problem Solving Evaluation	noted #	noted # # Page #		✓
				☐ Understands concepts and works with few errors
				☐ Understands concepts, but needs to reduce number of errors
				☐ Understands concepts, but percentage score reduced because of missing papers
				☐ Needs more practice with concepts presented
				☐ Needs more practice with concepts presented percentage score further reduced because of missing papers
				☐ Appropriate behavior

Teacher:

Comments:

Parent Signature _____

115

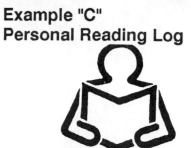

Rochester Public Schools
Rochester, Minnesota

Personal Reading Log

This log will help you record the books you read during the year. Hopefully, you will read more books than you list on this log. If so, after you have listed 50 books, write the **total** number of books read this year in the "Reading Star" at the end of this form. Then file your log in your STUDENT PROGRESS FOLDER.

Name _____   Grade _____

Kinds of Books: The symbol following each kind of book should be written under the column "Kind of Book."

Adventure (A)	**Folklore/Myths (FM)**	**Non-Fiction (N-F)**
Animal (An)	**Folk Tales (FT)**	**Poetry (P)**
Biography (B)	**Historical Fiction (HF)**	**Realistic Fiction (RF)**
Fantasy (Fa)	**Humorous (H)**	**Science Fiction (SF)**
Fiction (Fi)	**Mystery (M)**	**Sports (S)**

	Book Title	Author	Kind of Book
1.			
2.			
3.			
4.			
5.			
6.			
7.			
8.			
9.			
10.			
11.			
12.			
13.			
14.			
15.			
16.			
17.			
18.			
19.			
20.			
21.			

-OVER-

	Title	Author	Kind of Book
22.			
23.			
24.			
25.			
26.			
27.			
28.			
29.			
30.			
31.			
32.			
33.			
34.			
35.			
36.			
37.			
38.			
39.			
40.			
41.			
42.			
43.			
44.			
45.			
46.			
47.			
48.			
49.			
50.			

If you are a "Reading Star" and read more than 50 books, write the total number of books in the star below.

PARENT/GUARDIAN READING VERIFICATION FORM

Please assist your child by filling out a verification slip each time your son or daughter has completed a library book at home:

- -

(CUT HERE)

I VERIFY THAT _____ READ _____
             (Name of Child)   (Title of Library Book)

BY _____ SIGNED _____ DATE _____
    (Name of Author)   (Signature of Parent/Guardian)

- -

(CUT HERE)

I VERIFY THAT _____ READ _____
             (Name of Child)   (Title of Library Book)

BY _____ SIGNED _____ DATE _____
    (Name of Author)   (Signature of Parent/Guardian)

- -

(CUT HERE)

I VERIFY THAT _____ READ _____
             (Name of Child)   (Title of Library Book)

BY _____ SIGNED _____ DATE _____
    (Name of Author)   (Signature of Parent/Guardian)

- -

(CUT HERE)

I VERIFY THAT _____ READ _____
             (Name of Child)   (Title of Library Book)

BY _____ SIGNED _____ DATE _____
    (Name of Author)   (Signature of Parent/Guardian)

- -

(CUT HERE)

I VERIFY THAT _____ READ _____
             (Name of Child)   (Title of Library Book)

BY _____ SIGNED _____ DATE _____
    (Name of Author)   (Signature of Parent/Guardian)

- -

(CUT HERE)

PARENT/GUARDIAN READING VERIFICATION FORM

Please assist your child by filling out a verification slip each time your son or daughter has completed a library book at home:

- -
(CUT HERE)

I VERIFY THAT_____ **READ** _____
(Name of Child)   (Title of Library Book)

BY _____ **SIGNED** _____ **DATE** _____
(Name of Author)   (Signature of Parent/Guardian)

- -
(CUT HERE)

I VERIFY THAT_____ **READ** _____
(Name of Child)   (Title of Library Book)

BY _____ **SIGNED** _____ **DATE** _____
(Name of Author)   (Signature of Parent/Guardian)

- -
(CUT HERE)

I VERIFY THAT_____ **READ** _____
(Name of Child)   (Title of Library Book)

BY _____ **SIGNED** _____ **DATE** _____
(Name of Author)   (Signature of Parent/Guardian)

- -
(CUT HERE)

I VERIFY THAT_____ **READ** _____
(Name of Child)   (Title of Library Book)

BY _____ **SIGNED** _____ **DATE** _____
(Name of Author)   (Signature of Parent/Guardian)

- -
(CUT HERE)

I VERIFY THAT_____ **READ** _____
(Name of Child)   (Title of Library Book)

BY _____ **SIGNED** _____ **DATE** _____
(Name of Author)   (Signature of Parent/Guardian)

- -
(CUT HERE)

Name _____ Date _____

The Smile Report

Always   Sometimes   Never

 I am a good friend.

 I do my work neatly.

 I raise my hand.

 I follow directions carefully.

 I listen.

 I follow the rules.

 I walk quietly in the halls.

 I try my best.

Name _____   Date _____

Reading

DAP

PIc

Art

Music

Phy. Ed.

_____
Teacher's Name

Evaluation of Teacher by Student

DIRECTIONS: Put a ✔ on the correct ____.

	Yes:	No:	Don't Know:

1. Do you feel that I treat you fairly? 1) ____ ____ ____

2. Do you think that I try to make classwork fun or more interesting? 2) ____ ____ ____

3. Do I have a sense of humor? 3) ____ ____ ____

4. Am I too easy? (not strict enough) 4) ____ ____ ____

5. Am I too strict? 5) ____ ____ ____

6. Do I take enough interest in you personally? 6) ____ ____ ____

7. Am I patient and understanding enough? 7) ____ ____ ____

8. Is my voice clear and understanding enough? 8) ____ ____ ____

9. Do you think I expect too much from you? 9) ____ ____ ____

10. If something was bothering you, would you feel free to come to me about it? 10) ____ ____ ____

11. Do I make you nervous at times? 11) ____ ____ ____

12. Do you think I am friendly enough? 12) ____ ____ ____

13. If you could do it over again, would you choose this room for this grade? 13) ____ ____ ____

14. List something that you especially like about me or the way the classroom is run.

15. List something that you especially dislike about me or the way the classroom is run.

16. Which subject, that I have taught, have you liked the best?

17. Which subject, that I have taught, have you liked the least?

18. What are the three most important things you like to see in a teacher?

19. What grade would you give me? _____

20. Make any other comments you wish. (You can use the back.)

WRITING FOLDER

NAME_____

Skills Needed

Student	Teacher	
		Capitalize Titles
		Indent a Paragraph
		Indent all Paragraphs
		Use Periods at End of Sentences
		Contractions (')
		Quotation Marks (" ")
		Using Dictionary
		Cursive Writing
		Touch Margin
		Use of Commas in a List
		Dialogue-Indent every time a new person talks
		Capitalize "I"
		Don't start sentences with "And..."
		Period After Abbreviations
		Are/Our
		To/Two/Too
		A/An
		Proofreads for "known" skills

My Writing Record

Name_____ Date _____

Date	Title

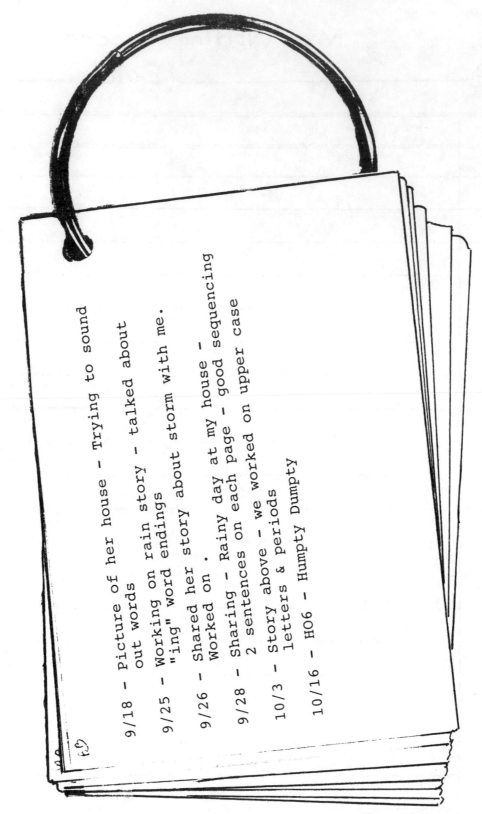

9/18 - Picture of her house - Trying to sound
out words

9/25 - Working on rain story - talked about
"ing" word endings
"ing" word story about storm with me.

9/26 - Shared her story about storm with me.
Worked on .

9/28 - Sharing - Rainy day at my house -
2 sentences on each page - good sequencing
we worked on upper case

10/3 - Story above - we worked on upper case
letters & periods

10/16 - HO6 - Humpty Dumpty

DAP Beginning Assessment

Name_____ Dates_____

1. Penny Game (Counting)
"Choose one group of pennies and find out how many there are in it. Do it so I can see you and hear you." (Repeat)

    4   8

    6   10 or 12

2. One-to-One Correspondence
(Make a row of 8 bottle tops. Give S 10 blue ones.) "Make a row of bottle tops beside my row of bottle tops so your row has the same number as mine."

O O O O O O O

3. Seriation
(Give S 12 straws from 5-15 cm. long; remove the 12 cm. and the 8 cm. straw; give remaining to S) "Can you put these in order from the longest to the shortest so they look like stairsteps?" (If S does, then give other straws to insert.) "Can you put this one in where it should go?"

    1. Does not order first set
    2. Orders first set
    3. Inserts (12 cm.) (8 cm.)

4. Making Collections
(Give S the set of paper shapes from the collections task or the set of felt shapes.) "Can you put the ones that go together; the ones that are alike in some way?"

    a. Graphic (lines, pairs, designs)
    b. Non-Graphic (groups by properties)

5. Order of Placement (topological space)
(Give S the set of beads and pipecleaners. Show S string of beads.) "Can you make a string of beads on your pipecleaner that looks just like mine?"

    a. Does not order beads
    b. Orders beads

6. Draw Yourself
    a. Scribbles
    b. "Newt" (head and limbs)
    c. Draws person (body, details)

7. Numeral Recognition

    0 1 2 3 4 5 6 7 8 9 10

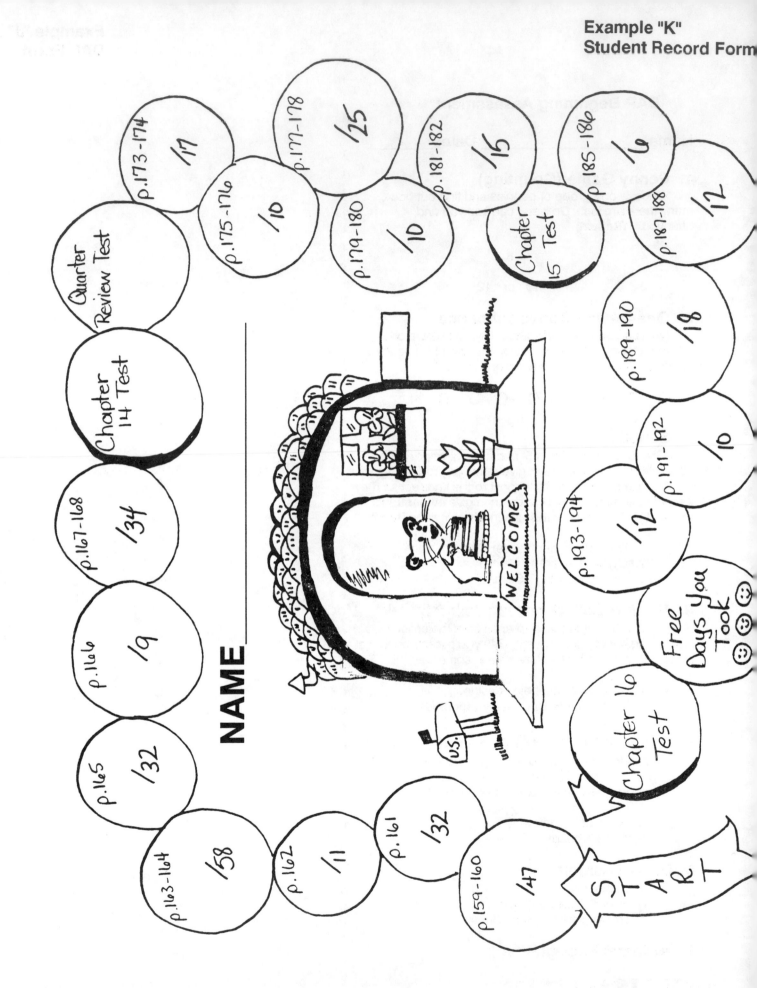

NAME

p.173-174 /17

p.175-176 /10

p.177-178 /25

p.179-180 /10

p.181-182 /15

p.185-186 /6

p.187-188 /12

Quarter Review Test

Chapter 15 Test

p.189-190 /18

Chapter 14 Test

p.191-92 /10

p.167-168 /34

p.193-194 /12

p.166 /9

Free Days You Took

p.165 /32

Chapter 16 Test

p.163-164 /58

p.162 /11

p.161 /32

p.159-160 /47

WELCOME

U.S.

START

ssessments

	1
	2
	3
	4
	5
	6
	7
	8
	9
	10
	11
	12
	13
	14
	15
	16
	17
	18
	19
	20
	21
	22
	23
	24
	25
	26
	27
	28
	29
	30
	31
	32
	33
	34
	35

Chapter VII - Time-savers and Fillers

TEACHER Please be aware that many of the ideas shared by teachers can
PLEASE and do transcend across several grade levels. Be sure to read
NOTE: all grades' suggestions in order to profit from the many other
excellent ideas.

INTRODUCTION

This chapter is filled with a rich selection of timesaving, practical suggestions to be used in many areas of your teaching.

There is never enough time in the day, month, or year to do everything you would like to do in teaching. Any time you save can be spent differently.

You have control of how you spend a large percentage of your time. To really improve your time management, you should go one step farther and do a time analysis as to how you spend a typical day and week. Use our three volumes of **Classroom Time Management** and their 24 chapters to guide your analysis.

NOTES:

"Yesterday's gone on down the river, and you can't

get it back."

--Larry McMurtry, Lonesome Dove
(Simon & Schuster)

**PARENT/
GUARDIAN
HELP ON
SPELLING**

Send home your master spelling list along with a "How to Study" sheet for parent/guardian to read. Also, give the tests for final assessment on Wednesdays, so that they always know when it will be, and you won't miss any due to having Fridays off once in awhile.
(See examples "A" and "B", pp. 156-156)

**WRITING
TO READ**

The IBM Corporation, 4111 Highway 52 North, Rochester, MN 55901, puts out a computer writing program called "Writing to Read." It fits into the Whole Language Approach, and can be used opposite a reading group, because it is self-directed and only needs two computers and two typewriters to set up.

**VISUAL
STORAGE**

Trace building blocks, glue bottles, and other items on paper. Attach these representations on the correct cabinets and drawers where these materials are stored. The visual will save the students, and you, a lot of time finding where to get and put things. Color coding game boxes helps students learn their colors while they are also organizing.

AVOID FRIDAY

A spelling schedule might be to introduce the list Monday, study a day or two, and test on Wednesday or Thursday.

BLOTTERS

Save time reteaching how to head papers and help keep desk tops clean. Make up permanent cardboard "blotters" for each child. At the top of the cardboard, print a model of how you want their papers to look. Under that, have an example of both lower and upper case letters to help students print their name correctly. The cardboard is larger than a regular piece of paper, so that any markers or crayons that drift off the paper will not go onto the desk but remain on the blotter. Cover them with contact paper or laminate for longer durability.

**CALENDAR
COUNTING**

Use different shapes, colors, or sizes for the numbers of your calendars. They can be used to show different sequences such as counting by 2's, 5's, 10's, etc.

S	M	T	W	TH	F	S
4	5	6	7	8	9	10

ROTATION

Teach rotation of station work at the same time you review shapes, colors, or numbers. Put the rotation order above each station. Laminate these cards for reuse. Pin a shape, color, or number on each student until they get the idea and can remember their group's designation. For example, the laminated cards might look like this:

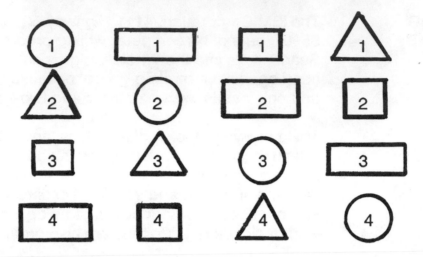

BOOKLETS

Booklets with student stories can be made with the help of older students. As a part of keyboarding, word processing for older students, they can type in the younger student's stories. The older ones will feel proud having helped the younger ones print and arrange a professional looking booklet for each to take home to share with parents.

BOOKMARK ASSIGNMENTS

Give students bookmarks. Mark missed assignments right on the bookmark. It acts as a reminder and as an assignment book. Put one in each textbook. Have students color one side so they have a positive investment for not losing them.

RAINY DAY

For a rainy day **"pick-me-up"** try keeping some clay in plastic bags. Cookie cutters, spools, and spoons to use to help keep their interest for long periods of time. It works great, when you have to stay in, due to inclement weather.

SELF-REMINDERS

Attach a clock face with glue, tape, or contact paper to the desks of students who leave the classroom for special help. If they can't tell time, they can match the hands with the classroom clock. You won't always have to be reminding them.

SUMMER STUDENT

Cut out and make all your birthday cards and hats for each child before school starts. Add their names to them during the first week of school. Always make some extras for new students. If you are absent, the sub will appreciate it, too.

LAMINATED BIRTHDAY CHART

Make up a laminated birthday chart. It may be one you add cutout cakes to with the students' names and dates.

PENCIL SHARPENING

When pencils need to be sharpened, put them in a box and a student will sharpen all of them after or before school. The names on the pencils allow them to be passed out quickly at the same time.

COLOR CODE READING BOOKS

Set up boxes or tubs with free reading materials color coded by subject. The books will get returned to the proper area without resorting. For example, an orange circle with a "H" on it might mean its an animal book/"H"ard level. A red circle with an "E" on it might mean its a people book/"E"asy level.

QUICK HIGH INTEREST

A quick, high interest, activity is to supply each student with a small amount of modeling clay in a plastic bag with a twistie. This is all they get, no additions when it's gone. They can make different letters, numbers, spell short words, make shapes, animals, or just be creative.

SEEDS

For an on-going sponge activity, for students who finish their work, give each a 35mm film can and as many bean seeds as it will hold. Students use this to help do their math, design creatively, or make shapes.

REUSED LESSON PLANS

Write separate lesson plans for each reading lesson in a spiral notebook. At the end of the year, you will have a complete set of lesson plans for each reading book. You will reap the time benefits next year by reusing them. Keep updating the lessons each year. A substitute or new teacher will thank you for sharing them. A paper clip makes it easy to find your place. Just number the lessons..

HELP EACH OTHER

Save lots of time, over a year, by cooperating together as teachers when taking and bringing classes to and from the special area teachers' rooms. Each takes his/her own class to the gym, for example, and brings the class that's finishing up back to their room. The next teacher will bring your class back for you when they deliver their class. Five minutes per day equals 2 1/2 total school days over just a 180 day period of time.

TEAMING PLANS

If you have a team at the primary level, divide up the total primary reading and math programs into generic lesson plans. Leave spaces to fill in specific pages and other important information needed. One time, long-range planning saves time. **(See examples "E", "F1", and "F2", pp. 160-162)**

PRE-TEST

Pre-testing will give you a sound basis for your teaching and save you many hours of teaching what they already know and can demonstrate. Those that test out can do enrichment, peer teaching, other subjects, personal reading time, extension work, research, etc.

INTEGRATE

Integrate curriculums. Teach spelling and handwriting together. Expect anything taught to be used effectively in all areas, not just when you're teaching it. Creative writing is a natural across all curriculum areas. In other words, writing about science kills two birds with one stone; buying you time and satisfying a more demanding curriculum.

STRETCH SPELLING LIST

Also, you may develop stretch spelling lists from students' own misspellings, reading level vocabulary words, or any other subject area. These are best used with students who can handle enrichment activities. **(See example "I", p. 165)**

STUDENT RECORD

Make up and run many copies of a master chart with class list chart with many check-off boxes behind each name. Students can color in a square under the proper heading when they bring in a permission slip, assignment, art material, lunch count, etc. It is a quick visual reference to spot who needs what. Best of all, you do not have to do the recording. **(See example on next page.)**

STUDENT RECORD CHART

NAME	Math #1	Art	Speech #1	Math #2	Field Trip	
Joey Brown						
John Merrill						
Mary Samson						
Barbara Webber						

"CATS"

Introduce the 4 types of sentences with the acronym: "CATS."

C = Command

A = Asking

T = Telling

S = Surprise or exclamation

Remind them to add a variety of types of sentences in their writings with the word CATS on their papers.

STUDENT WRITING BOOKLET

Save time by making a blank form for student writing. Leave a blank space at the top for an illustration and use penmanship paper for the written lines at the bottom. Run off enough copies for the semester/year. Colored paper is a nice variation. They can be easily laminated and put into booklets. **(See example "L", p. 168)**

NOTES:

"*Dost thou love life? Then do not squander time,*

for that's the stuff life is made of."

Benjamin Franklin
1706 - 1790
Poor Richard's Almanack

SHARPENING TIME

Be sure to have the students bring **SHARPENED** pencils to school the first day. Emphasize this on "Meet the Teacher Day" before school starts, and put it prominently on the supply request lists. This will eliminate a lot of noise confusion and down-time on the first day of school.

Also, each child may bring 6-7 pencils with their names on the pencils. When they need sharpening, they put theirs in the **"sharpening box."** A student has the job of sharpening the pencils before or after school.

SELF-ADHESIVE LABELS

Use computer-printed pre-gummed labels printed with each student's name on. Keep labels on a clipboard, write notes on the labels about student speeches, presentations, etc. Simply peel off and attach to their work, your grade book, their desk, their project, etc.

SEATING

A quick way to change desk arrangement is to put the blank grid on a transparency, which has a blank seating chart. Call on students to give you a coordinate of where they would best learn. Discuss choices and write in their initials on a transparency as you go. Students then move their desks to their new position when told to do so.

Example of transparency:

```
                    ┌──────────┐
                    │ Teacher's│
                    │   Desk   │
                    └──────────┘

         A      B      C      D      E      F

   1.    □      □      □      □      □      □


   2.    □      □      □      □      □      □


   3.    □      □      □      □      □      □
```

OVERHEAD

Rethink the use of your overhead projector. What if you set it on the bottom drawer of your desk? It will be about desk height. Have the screen behind you and teach from your desk. You will have better eye contact with the students, than using the chalkboard. The writing is easier for the students to see. Your transparency files can be right in the drawer. Develop maps, all answer keys, vocabulary, spelling lists, etc.

(Time-savers and Fillers)

OVERHEAD CONT'D — for the files. Colored pens work great for emphasis. Easy clean up and less paper shuffling make it something to think seriously about.

For pre-test spelling, check by using the overhead. The student writes the word the way he/she think it is spelled. The class evaluates and checks their own papers as they go, starring the ones they need to study for the upcoming post-test for grade. A major advantage is that you can "read" the students' reactions as you face them, versus having your back to them while writing on the chalkboard.

For post-test spelling, students can self-check or check a partner's paper from the key displayed on the overhead projector. It is one more time they are dealing with the words and you don't have as much correcting to do.

PROOFING — Put proofreading sentences on transparencies. It will save you time writing them on the board each time. The corrections can be shown in different colors and wiped off for the next use.

BOOK REPORTS — Save time reviewing student library book reading. Have them give oral reports to the class. The students may vote on their favorite story. This is an easy promotional program and elicits accountability. It also relates to reporting in front of a group.

READING CHECK — Develop a short matching exercise for each story in the reading text. It raises comprehension and checks to see how well they read the selection. It sets another purpose for reading carefully.

"GROUP" AGENDA — Post a class meeting or circle group agenda for anyone to add to throughout the week. If a problem arises, have the student write it down for quality discussion and solution.

P.E. SHOES — Have students put on gym shoes during their snack break, when they come in at noon hour, or any other time when it won't take away from the immediate physical education time.

IMPORTANT ITEMS — Write things of importance on the board, the night before, to eliminate that behind feeling you get, when the principal calls an unexpected meeting at 8:00 A.M.

SHARING TIME

Have students sign up for sharing times ahead. This limits the number of students and means some forethought has gone into the request. Keep a checklist so that a few do not monopolize the privilege.

MAPS

Make maps on large, clear, vinyl plastic. Using permanent markers, trace the maps on "backwards" using an overhead projector. Students can lay them flat on the floor with the tracings on the underside. Using overhead marking pens, students can mark in boundaries, rivers, cities, mountains, countries, etc. Wash off, and reuse for many years.

TEACH MATERIALS WHEREABOUTS

Save time by not having to constantly give out materials or tell students where they are. Have a full discussion about materials, there whereabouts (leave them out to see), and students' responsibility. This early lesson will save you many small discussions, and students will have the lessons of dependability and independence.

PRETEST "NEEDS"

Focus your time on areas of "need." Pre-test, teach to those needs, and only re-test on the areas they did not master on the pre-test. Blanket coverage looks easier at first glance; however, it is inefficient and destroys morale for those who already know the material.

SPELLING TEST

If you have two classes of the same grade level, set a time to give your spelling tests as a combined group. This will free up one of you every other time for preparation.

TEST ON CASSETTE

Put all your spelling tests on cassette tape with background music. You can do something else while students take the test. Students who were absent can self test at noon, or another time. You can reinforce the music program by discussing the composer and music selection. Once on tape, the spelling program is good for the duration of your present spelling series--years.

READING LIBRARY

Develop your own library from Reader's Digest. Copy and laminate the books at the end of each month's magazine. Since you have already read them, you can better introduce them and hold a meaningful discussion.

EFFECTIVE STORAGE

Store all reading materials next to the reading table. Put other materials near where they will be used most. Have **"a place for everything and everything in its place"** is a <u>very</u> relevant saying.

X-RAY SHEETS

Get clear X-ray sheets to make covers for reading plan sheets, etc. They allow you to see both sides and protect the papers with a durable cover.

DISCUSSION VS PAPERWORK

Do some lessons every day that result in no papers to be corrected.

1. After reading a story in the basal reader, ask comprehension questions for students to answer orally. Use higher level thinking questions such as:

   - "Do you agree with that answer?"
   - "Who can give me another answer to that question?"
   - "Can you prove that?"
   - "Why is that a good answer?"

2. After reading a story, have students write three questions about the story. Hold a discussion during which students get to ask their questions, and call on someone to answer.

3. Make up sets of flashcards for words with math problems. Let students work with a partner and test one another.

EDITING

Use and teach Editing Marks. These symbols are quick and easy to use when correcting writings. It comes from <u>Language for Daily Use</u>, Phoenix Edition, Harcourt, Brace, and Javanovich Publishers.

COOPERATIVE ROLES

Use a grid square to easily keep track of roles assigned to cooperative learning groups. A class list or a short grid with just the group's names on can be used to assign the roles an equal number of times throughout the year. Students keep track of this themselves and put it in their group's folder. **(See example "N", p. 171)**

SHORT SHOTS

Put **Short Shots** proofreading sentences on the overhead and on handouts. Do two sentences a day. After the student is finished writing them, with their corrections, a partner corrects it using the overhead as a key. **(See example "H", p. 164)**

QUICK EVALUATION FORM FOR WRITINGS

Use a three-prong evaluation technique for writings: The writer, the peers, and the teacher. A quick, short 12-question evaluation form can be rated with numbers 1-2-3. **(see example "D", p. 159)**

FLASH CARDS

Put math flash cards on a ring. Check the facts off on a chart as they are accomplished. Recycle them so they become part of their long-term memory.

STUDENTS' BOOK SHELF

You don't have to wait for students to find the correct textbook in a messy desk. Build, or have built, a book shelf three slots wide and ten slots high. These thirty spaces can be fit into a three foot by five foot space and 18 inches deep. Desks will be more functional, and the textbooks will always be easy to find.

SPELLING LISTS

An excellent, quick way to give extension work to high potential pupils is to assign special spelling lists made up from reading vocabulary, science units being studied, etc. **(See example "I", p. 165)**

SOURCE FOR MAKING BOOKS

An excellent source on how to more efficiently make books with children comes from:

How to Make Books with Children

Teacher's Resource Book Level 1-6
By Joy Evans and Ho Ellen Moore
12417 26th Avenue N.
Plymouth, MN 55441
(612) 553-1575

NOTES:

"*Everything looks impossible for the people who never try anything.*"

--*Jean-Louis Etienne*

BAR GRAPH/ SPELLING

Integrate bar graphing with spelling by having the students record their own test scores on a bar graph for each unit. Students can also graph their own height and weight each month.

COMPUTER STORAGE

Save time and space. Put your best lesson/units on a computer disc. Also keep your "master" worksheets there. You won't need those big file cabinets. Just run off a copy from the word processor and make copies of worksheets on the copy machine.

CHART PERCENTAGES

If you figure percentages for grading papers and tests, figure them out only once, and make a list based on the total number of points. Save this with the test, or cover it with clear contact paper on the outside of a folder. The next time, you will just have to look at the chart, and the percentages will already have been figured upon the total points possible.

REVIEW BY GROUPS

Use cooperative group learning to review material. It is twice as fast, involves more students, goes into more depth than whole class review, and is motivating.

TIME TO GIVE EXTRA HELP

Developing independent study packets for top, self-directed students will allow extra time for you to work with those students needing more direct attention.

ASKING QUESTIONS

Teach your children to be problem solvers and self-sufficient. Give them these four steps, to take in sequence, when faced with a question normally taken to you first:
1) look for answers from themselves
2) look for answers from materials such as texts and reference books
3) look to peers and others
4) last resort, see the teacher. This will cut down the number of time-draining interruptions.

BOOK REPORTS

A unique way of giving book reports is with the video camera. Partners select a book each wants to read. They develop a report which is videotaped for the total class to review. The report is about three minutes long and includes a discussion and comparing of viewpoints.

STUDENT SELECTION   Have student names on small, permanent cards. These can be used for job rotation or to call on students when you want to insure everyone has an equal chance or choice. Shuffle them for random order or keep them alphabetical. How about <u>two</u> sets?

DAILY NEWS   For discussing daily news, have permanent headings listed on the board. Then just write in the answers underneath as the article is discussed. Typical headings could be: Who, What, When, Where, Why, How, and impact on the variables of Social, Economical, Political, Technological, Environmental, Cultural, etc.

PERCENTAGES LISTED   Copy the scores and percentages of different, often-used assessments. Tape these under plastic for durability. Put them on subject folders for easy reference. You won't have to figure percentages again. You may want to put these various computations all on one sheet in your grade book, too. **(See example "K", p. 167)**

FIGURE PERCENTAGES   Figure percentages instantly with "Easy Grader." This slide rule figures percentages, for as few as eight answers or as many as 95 answers. It is made by **Slide Chart, Perry Graft, Los Angeles, CA 91324-3552; Stock #5703.** It also can be purchased from St. Paul Book Store in St. Paul, MN.

QUOTATIONS   If you don't want to search for quotes for committee work, for teacher-designed tests and worksheets, for teaching, or for putting up in your room, save time by simply purchasing **The New International Dictionary of Quotations**. It sells for about $4.50, is copyrighted in 1986, and is co-authored by Hugh Rowson and Margaret Miner. It is published through: Nat Penguin, Inc., 1633 Broadway, New York, NY 10019.

SKILLS OF INDEPENDENCE   Teach skills of independence. Establish routines for students so that you do not have to keep giving directions for things you do all year long. You will be buying lots of extra productive time for the rest of the year.

DAILY ROUTINE   Get yourself into a daily, specific routine as soon as possible. You will not waste as much time, and it will gain time for you to be more productive--planning, for correcting papers, or for whatever.

PERSONAL NOTES Purchase rubber stamps targeted to your personal needs. Any notes, that you often repeat on papers, should be on a stamp. Have a student even do the stamping. This saves a lot of time, and looks neater, too. Examples might be: PLEASE SIGN AND RETURN, SAVE, PRETEST, POST-TEST, REDO AND HAND BACK IN, etc.

START ON TIME The best time-saver of all is to **start on time**. A fast start after the bell saves 5-10 minutes each time. Remember, five minutes saved each day for 180 school days is equal to 2 1/2 **total** school days!

GETTING MATERIALS Do not lay out any materials. Teach all students to get their own materials, clean up, and put materials away responsibly. Teach skills of independence to buy you lots of time later.

CLEAN TABLES Cut large plastic sheets to cover each table or desk. They are easy to wipe off and hang to dry. No more glue or magic marker to clean off desk tops. Reuse indefinitely.

PAPER SCRAPS Have a scrap box for all paper. Reuse for lots of things. Don't forget that both sides of the paper can be used. Recycling is always appropriate for budget and environmental purposes.

LOST AND FOUND If you spend time with lost items, finding out who owns what, and telling students to pick up things off the floor, help is here. Develop a lost and found box. Any item out of place goes in it automatically. Students go there first instead of asking you where a misplaced item is. Students may decorate the box, and think of a "catchy" name like "Davey Jone's Locker."

QUALITY PRODUCTS Whatever you develop (whether a form, certificate, poster, or game), make a **"quality"** product. You will reuse it and save time redoing it over and over. Do it right the first time.

MAGNETS ON THE CHALKBOARD Did you know that magnets stick to chalkboards, just like they do to refrigerators? They are faster than tape, and do not leave the sticky marks. Some magnets even come with hooks.

HANGING STUDENTS' WORK	Run a wire, across the end of the room next to a wall where it will be out of the way. Put it at student height. Students can hang up and take down their own art projects and papers. The display can easily be changed continuously without you ever touching it. Clothespins work well as attachments. You save time and other bulletin board space.
NUMBERS VS NAMES	Don't find yourself relabeling coat hall hooks, mailboxes, etc. each year. Put numbers on them once and reassign them each year by corresponding number from your class list.
AREA OF NEED	When going over tests or papers that have already been corrected, just note the problem areas, don't go over the areas already mastered. Ask, "who has a question on #1, #2, #3, ...?"
BEFORE SCHOOL STARTS	Run off all packets and as many materials as possible before school starts in the fall. There will be less sense of urgency, and you won't have to go through the same steps over and over again all year long. Label the files so students can readily see chapter materials and become more self-directed.
PAPER TIGER	The "Paper Tiger" is the name of the Rochester's district's central duplicating division. It is used to run off copies of 30 or more, with a turn around time of two to three days. It reproduces, collates, punches, staples, etc. These processes take up a lot of your time, when they could be done by district help. Run off everything for the year ahead of time. Just file it and don't spend time waiting for the building-level duplicating machine.
DIE CUTTER	The "Die Cutter" is a lifesaver for doing bulletin boards and lettering. It is a hand/lever machine which comes with different sized letters, numerals, and patterns. You can cut out multiple copies of any of these with just one pull of the lever. It works well to laminate colored paper before you cut out the pattern. Can be purchased from:

Ellison Educational
P.O. Box 7986
Newport Beach, CA 92658-0986
Telephone (714) 646-4496

**DAP
PUTTY**

Most discount/variety stores carry a product called **"DAP."** It is a putty-like product, used in place of masking tape to adhere things to the wall. It may be used over and over without leaving marks on the wall. It is fast to just tear off a chunk and press on.

**EXTRA
COPIES**

ALWAYS run off a few extra copies of any worksheet, newsletter, bulletin, etc. You won't find yourself running to make that extra copy for the student who lost his/her copy, needs to redo, wants an extra, etc.

**SCANNER
TO SCORE
TESTS**

Use a scanner to score tests. This machine uses pre-made bubble sheet forms to record answers to tests. The machine scores, shows analysis, and is easy to use.

**LAP
CHALKBOARDS**

Use small lap chalkboards. They provide checks for understanding with 100% involvement. Students write their individual answers and hold them up for you to check.

**SCRATCH
PAPER**

Use a lap-size chalkboard or notebook-size scratch paper to do a math problem on. The students hold up their work when done. The teacher can scan the class for an immediate check for understanding without going to each desk. Less reteaching will be needed later.

The title is **The New International Dictionary of Quotations** and is copyrighted 1986.

**TRAFFIC
PATTERN**

Don't get into a set traffic pattern in your building which might not be the most efficient. Make a conscious effort to analyze your building, and choose the shortest route to different areas. This will save you extra travel time, steps, and energy.

(Time-savers and Fillers)

NEW TEACHER New teachers should find a reliable teacher at your grade level to help you learn the ropes. What are the building's high priorities, where are materials found, what procedures have to be followed, etc.?

REFERENCE BOOK Keep a request list of reference books needed from the library, to pull, which correlate with each of your units. Just hand in the prewritten request list to the librarian a few days ahead of when you will need them.

CHILD'S NAME ON Send a reminder note and repeated reminders that childrens' names must be on <u>all</u> materials brought to school. The beginning of the year supply list is a "natural" for this information, also.

HOLD PAGES OPEN Use very large paper clips or purchased clips to hold workbook and teacher texts to the pages you're using. In this way you do not have to page through to find the pages you're working on each day.

TEACHER'S EDITION Mark all the edges of your teacher's editions with magic marker. They can be located much more quickly, and makes them easy to see who is using them.

TELEPHONE CALLS Save all your return telephone calls until after school, and do them all at one time. Don't take normal calls during teaching times. Instruct the secretary to take a message unless it is an emergency.

SIGN ON DOOR Use a sign on your door to buy time and limit interruptions. Examples:

"TESTING - Please do not disturb."

"INSTRUCTIONAL LESSON - Please do not interrupt."

"DOING MY WORK - Please do not interrupt."

COMPUTER NEWSLETTERS Do parent newsletters on the computer. The word processor allows you to make corrections before printing out the final copy. Long hand and typing mistakes can take a lot of extra time.

VOLUNTEERS   Parent volunteers are good "P.R." and time-savers. If you can delegate, without feeling no one can do as good a job as you, and are confident in your professional delivery, organize parent volunteers. They can save you unlimited work, help you deliver more quality to the students, and give you support. Start small and work up to your comfort level.

LIBRARY SKILLS   With flexible library scheduling and cooperation, the reading teacher, librarian, and classroom teacher can make a team effort to teach library skills, language arts skills, and curriculum. Three teachers with one class is concentrated efficiency.

STUDENT TEACHER   Request for a student teacher. You will see new methods, units, and ideas. Two teachers, for the same number of students, can have extra time to get around to all students more often. Dividing up the teaching gives extra planning time.

SENIOR CITIZENS   Explore the possibilities of getting senior citizens to help you as volunteers in the school. Everyone benefits. Grandparents have the time, love, and willingness to be **"grand"** helpers.

TEAMING   Team teachers should divide up the duties. Rotate the jobs of newsletter, unit planning, break monitor, film projectionist, etc. Share films with another teacher. One teacher is responsible for the two classes: introduction, showing, and follow-up discussion. Take turns. This gives the second teacher planning time.

ART PROJECT   Have parent volunteers or teaching assistants paper clip materials together for each student to use for an art project. Handing out the little packet will save countless minutes in organizing and off-task activity.

CALLING VOLUNTEERS   Use a room parent volunteer to help make calls for other volunteers. This will save you calling all the parents to get help for various projects. Supply them with a directory of names and telephone numbers for your class.

COOPERATIVE UNIT

Save planning time by dividing up units. For example, if three teachers each teach the same unit to all three classrooms, on a rotational basis, the curriculum is covered more efficiently. Also, you are forced to stay within set time lines. This self-imposed expectation will, in itself, make you more efficient to finish the unit on time instead of letting it it drag on.

SWITCH CLASSES

Switch a class with another teacher, so that you exchange students. You teach the same lesson twice, once for your students, and then switch classes and teach the same lesson to the other class. You will save making out one lesson plan each time. Teach to your <u>strengths</u> and <u>interests</u>.

REUSABLE NOTES

Develop reusable parent notes for reoccurring needs in the classroom. For example, parent permission slips, need for glue, pencils, etc., announcements of yearly projects, and anything else that would be repeated in the future. Keep them in a file so that you don't have to keep repeating the procedure. Leave blanks for the dates if they are needed. Then just fill in the date on one sheet and run off copies. **(See example "J", p. 166)**

COMMITTEES

Keep in mind that committee work outside the classroom will draw down your energies. Don't volunteer unless you are truly committed to the cause, and are conscious of the time you will be spending on it.

MAIL

Screen your teacher's mail immediately as you get it out of your mailbox. Throw 3rd class mail and any 2nd class mail you do not need. Check and dump all non important information, so that you do not have to carry it around or look at it ever again. The rest goes back to the room, dates written down on a master calendar and the memo/paper thrown away. It is easier to keep up with the paper blizzard than to let it stack up and get overwhelming later.

WHO IS DOING THE WORK

Don't do anything for students that they can do for themselves. It is always quicker in the short run to do it yourself, and get it done right the first time. However, you will be doing it over and over again in the future, unless you teach and expect the student to learn routine, run errands, and think for themselves. Then sit back and watch it happen.

LONG-RANGE PLANNING

Before school starts in the fall, plan long range with a large sheet of paper divided into months. Color code subject areas. Put in all required units, chapters, curriculum, etc. This will give you a structured goal to aim for, and provides a quick check to see the total picture anytime during the year. Save to readjust for the next year. **(See example "G", p. 163)**

LESSON PLAN FILE

Build a teaching file of lesson plans. As you read or think of ideas from any source, start to fill in a "blank" lesson plan form. Sometimes you will only fill in the first part or the end of a lesson. Fill in the details later, but the idea is captured during the moment and you don't have to recopy it onto a lesson plan form later.
(See examples "M1" and "M2", pp. 169-170)

WEEKLY HOMEWORK READER

Make out a homework sheet for each week's reading. They are used over each year. Give them out once a week for increased parent involvement, student involvement, and to reinforce the reading taught in the room.
(See example "C", p. 158)

WEEKLY READING SHEETS

A quick, complete sketch of the week's reading plans for each group can be put on reusable blanks. It is invaluable for a substitute teacher, and keeps you well planned. Tape them right in your plan book or keep them with your reading materials. **(See example "O", p. 172)**

REUSABLE PLANS

Using legal sized paper, write out day-by-day plans for each unit. Add all handouts, film numbers, resources, etc. It can be reorganized easily and kept year after year. Don't redo units all over again each year!

STUDENT INFORMATION

Save lots of time by making a master list of students, their addresses, their birthdays, and their telephone numbers. Do this within the first two weeks of school. Don't wait for a list from the office which will be incomplete, anyway. Put this information in your plan book for ready reference.

UNITS ORGANIZED INTO FOLDERS

Separate subject units into file folders, so you can quickly add any additional supportive materials that you used outside of the curriculum. Jot notes on the file folder about
    a. resource people
    b. library books
    c. films used
    d. art projects

PRIORITIES   Keep a priority list. Realize that you cannot do everything, so just do the most important things first. Keep a list of things to do for next year.

STAFF MEETING Encourage your principal to put **"sharing"** on the staff meeting agenda. Teachers need time to share ideas, materials, etc. This is a positive part of the meeting and peer coaching does make a difference.

"Lost time is never found again."

Benjamin Franklin

MUSIC

Use music as a "filler" between activities. When a number of students are through with a task, start to sing. Those done join in. When everyone is through, you sing one song and then give directions for the next lesson/activity.

3 x 5 CARDS

Keep individual student's writing records (and others) on 3 x 5 note cards punched in a corner and put on a snap ring to keep them alphabetical. **(See example "I", p. 122)**

VISUAL MEMORY

Display a large picture for 2-3 minutes. Remove the picture and ask questions about what they remember seeing in the picture. Have them write about it. Memory work can be compared to being a detective, or a witness to a crime.

20 QUESTIONS

Play the game 20 questions. Think of an object in the room. They can ask questions answerable by only "yes" or "no." If they want to guess, they stand up. If they guess wrong, they are out of that game. The winner takes the teacher's place to think of an object. There is a lot of thinking strategy involved, and listening skills are a "must." If the object isn't guessed after 20 questions, the teacher wins and thinks of another object.

NOTES:

"Change, like sunshine, can be a friend or a foe, a

blessing or a curse, a dawn or a dusk."

--William Arthur Ward

RIDDLES/ POEMS

Have students prepare a riddle or poem to be given if students get ready quickly for the next subject, etc.

On Friday hand out 5 riddle slips:

MON-Riddle, TUE-Riddle, WED-Riddle, TH-Riddle, FRI-Riddle

Also hand out 5 poem slips:

MON-Poem, TUE-Poem, WED-Poem, TH-Poem, FRI-Poem

Students are to be prepared to give theirs on the given day.

STATIONS WHEN FINISHED

Set up learning stations to go to when work is finished. Ideas include computer, math games, jigsaw puzzles, worksheets with crosswords and fun color sheets, listening station with headsets, filmstrip previewers, art work, etc.

7-UP GAME

The game of 7-up is fun and quiet. Choose "seven people to be up." The rest put their heads down and their thumbs up. The seven chosen then go out and gently put one classmate's thumbs down. When all seven have returned to the front, the ones with thumbs down get one guess as to who chose them. If they are correct, they trade places with the one that was up.

SILENT MATH

Do silent math with your class. It works for addition, subtraction, multiplication and division. It is a perfect activity when you are waiting in line or for a moment or two before the bell rings. The teacher holds up a number of fingers, makes an operation sign (+ - X -), holds up a number of fingers, and makes an equal sign. Students also respond with finger numbers.

MAP LOCATIONS

Map location activity: Make up 100 or more names of countries (one per slip). Two teams play this each morning for two minutes. One student, per team, per day, participates for the running score by drawing out a name and having one minute to find it on a large pull-down map. (At the end of 30 seconds, the player who cannot find it may have one hint from one of his/her team members as to which continent the country is in.) The beauty of this is that students look at the country names and check where they are on their own time throughout the school year. Global education in just two minutes a day. (Variation: Use states.)

152

NOTES:

"There are no secrets to success. It is the result of preparation, hard work, learning from failure."

--Gen. Collin L. Powell in The Black Collegian

VIDEOTAPE SPEECHES

Videotape all student speeches and special presentations. When the class has to stay in at noon, play the video back to hold the students' interest for long periods of time.

TRIP

Say, "I'm going on a trip and I'll take a _____." Students keep adding items, one at a time, in alphabetical order. Alphabetical order by first letter of the item is the key to be able to add an item.

FILLER

Make a teacher "Time Out" drawer. Arrange it by subject areas and use when you need a filler for 10-20 minutes or as a real change of pace. Games, puzzles, stories, brain teasers, etc. work well. The substitute teacher can use them, too. Be sure to date the back of them after using so you don't repeat them in the same school year (unless, of course, they were requested due to popular demand.)

SPELLING

Spelling Basketball: Students are given the spelling list to study one night in advance, knowing that the next day is **Spelling Basketball**. Two teams line up. Tape a line for 2 points and another further away for 3 points. If the first person spells a word correctly, he/she gets a chance to shoot a nerf ball into the wastebasket from the line of their choice. Alternate back and forth, keeping a running score on the board.

CRAZY ANNIE

Crazy Annie: The teacher starts by saying: "I have a friend. Her name is Annie, and she likes _____, but does not like _____." Fill in the blanks with something like: "She likes the Mississippi River, but does not like the Nile. The next student says: "She likes the Mississippi River, but does not like _____," filling in the blank with a word that does not have the pattern you are thinking of. When several students have tried different combinations, whoever thinks they know the clue you are thinking of may stand up and guess. If they are right, they get to start a new one. If wrong, they are out of the game. The clue in the above example would be a double letter word. It might be starting letters, vowel pattern, ending letter, subject, etc. It reinforces listening and thinking skills, much like the game 20 Questions.

"Experience isn't interesting until it begins to

repeat itself -- in fact, until it does that, it hardly

is experience."

Elizabeth Bowen

HOW TO STUDY
SPELLING
WORDS

Children benefit from a consistent method in learning
how to study spelling words. The following procedure
will be used in the spelling program and should be
taught, retaught, and reviewed at every grade level.
Teachers are encouraged to print the procedure on a
chart, which is then placed in the classroom where
all children can refer to it.

HOW TO STUDY A WORD

STEP 1: LOOK at the word
carefully.

STEP 2: SAY the word aloud.

STEP 3: CLOSE your eyes and see the
word as you spell it to
yourself.

STEP 4: COVER the word and then
write it.

STEP 5: CHECK the spelling (If the
word is misspelled, return
to STEP 1.)

Credit to: Independent School District
Rochester, Minnesota
Language Arts Department

SPELLING TEST

NAME_____UNIT____DATE_____

BASIC   STRETCH

1._____   1._____

2._____   2._____

3._____   3._____

4._____   4._____

5._____   5._____

6._____   6._____

7._____   7._____

8._____   8._____

9._____   9._____

10._____   10._____

11._____   11._____

12._____   12._____

13._____   13._____

14._____   14._____

15._____   15._____

16._____   16._____

17._____   17._____

18._____   18._____

19._____   19._____

20._____   20._____

21._____   21._____

22._____   22._____

23._____   23._____

24._____   24._____

25._____   25._____

Homework - Jan. 12,

<u>Vocabulary</u> - Read each word. Use each word in a sentence and illustrate.

eat   fish   dolphin

<u>Draw</u> - On the paper attached, draw a real animal and a make-believe animal.

<u>Decoding</u> - Read each word. If the vowel has the sound of "e" as in jeep, circle the word. If the vowel has the sound of "e" as in hen, color the word.

beet   ten   pep   meet   bet
met   teen   feed   fed   wed
weed   peep   bed   heel   pen

<u>Read</u>. Read the phrases attached. Read "A Bell for the Cat."

Parent signature   * Return Monday, Jan. 15

EVALUATION FORM:

Writer _____   Date_____

Title_____   Evaluator_____

Circle One: UNFINISHED   FINAL COPY

Evaluation Scale:

The Writer's Scale:
1. I want to work more on this.
2. This is all right.
3. I'm very happy with this.

Teacher/Peer Opinion
1. Please show this to me again
   after you've worked on it.
2. This is all right.
3. You should be very happy
   with it.

	The Writer's Opinion -- 1, 2, or 3	Peer Group Opinion -- 1, 2, or 3	Teacher's Opinion -- 1, 2, o
IDEAS:			
1. Is the writing interesting? Is the topic a good one?			
2. Does the writing make sense? Are the ideas in good order?			
3. Does it show imagination?			
4. Is it something the reader can picture? Does it show...not just tell?			
5. Is it written to the right audience?			
6. Is there variety in the sentence structure?			
7. If there is dialogue, is it realistic?			
8. Should more deatils be added?			
9. Is the problem a good one?			
10. Are the characters believable?			
11. Does the beginning "hook" the reader?			
12. Is the ending satisfactory? Does the protagonist solve the problems?			

Teacher's Evaluation
--1, 2, or 3

MECHANICS: (teacher grades final copy only)

1. Is the form correct?	
2. Is the grammar correct?	
3. Are capital letters used correctly?	
4. Are all punctuation marks used correctly?	
5. Are all words spelled correctly?	
6. Is the handwriting clear and readable?	

REMARKS/SUGGESTIONS:

Bobcats

Level 8 - Give Me a Clue

Title The Wolf in the Wool Suit pp. 262-2?

1. Prepare Rdg. p   T.G. 263
2. Rdg. Comp. p. 134-138 T.G. 264-269
        Silent Rdg.
        Oral Rdg.
3. Developing Rdg. Skills | PP 269-271 T.G. |

———————————————————————

Assign Skillpack
    p.p. 77, 78, 79, 80
Correct Skillpack
    pp. 77, 78, 79, 80
4. Ext. Rdg. Skills | PP 272 T.G. |

Title Turkey Girl   pp. 273-28?

1. Prepare Rdg. p   T.G 274
2. Rdg. Comp. p. 139-145 T.G. 275-282
        Silent Rdg.
        Oral Rdg
3. Developing Rdg. Skills | PP 282-285 T.G |

———————————————————————

Assign Skillpack
    pp. 81, 82, 83, 84, 85
Correct Skillpack
    pp. 81, 82, 83, 84, 85
4. Ext. Rdg. Skills | PP 286-287 T.G. |

Mathematics

Day _____   Students needing extra help:

Correct p. _____

Discussion p. _____
Materials needed:

Assignment p. _____

- -

_____   Students needing extra help:

Correct p. _____

Discussion p. _____
Materials needed:

Assignment p. _____

- -

          Students needing extra help:

_____

Correct p. _____

Discussion p. _____
Materials needed:

Assignment p. _____

- -

          Students needing extra help:

_____

Correct p. _____

Discussion p. _____
Materials needed:

Assignment p. _____

- -

          Students needing extra help:

_____

Correct p. _____

Discussion p. _____
Materials needed:

Assignment p. _____

Reading Lesson Plans

MONDAY

Teacher's Edition   p.

Chart   p.

Text   p.

Skills   p.

TUESDAY

Teacher's Edition   p.

Chart   p.

Text   p.

Skills   p.

WEDNESDAY

Teacher's Edition   p.

Chart   p.

Text   p.

Skills   p.

THURSDAY

Teacher's Edition   p.

Chart   p.

Text   p.

Skills   p.

FRIDAY

Teacher's Edition   p.

Chart   p.

Text   p.

Skills   p.

Reading Lesson Plans

MONDAY

Teacher's Edition   p.

Chart   p.

Text   p.

Skills   p.

TUESDAY

Teacher's Edition   p.

Chart   p.

Text   p.

Skills   p.

WEDNESDAY

Teacher's Edition   p.

Chart   p.

Text   p.

Skills   p.

THURSDAY

Teacher's Edition   p.

Chart   p.

Text   p.

Skills   p.

FRIDAY

Teacher's Edition   p.

Chart   p.

Text   p.

Skills   p.

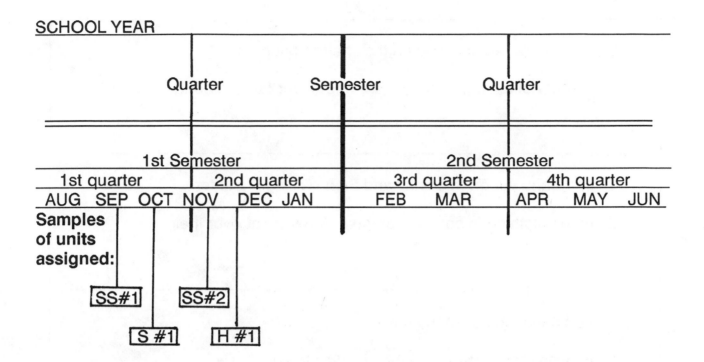

SCHOOL YEAR

	Quarter		Semester		Quarter		

1st Semester		2nd Semester	
1st quarter	2nd quarter	3rd quarter	4th quarter
AUG SEP OCT NOV DEC JAN		FEB MAR	APR MAY JUN

Samples of units assigned:

SS#1   SS#2

S #1   H #1

Add in as you long-range plan.

Conference	= red
Vacation	= blue
Field Trips	= green
Any specific deadline	= yellow

Add in as you long range plan.

Units   SS#1

Code by
Subject Area   SS#1   (Social Studies)

"   "   S #1   (Science)

"   "   H #1   (Health)

**NOTE: This long-range planning form needs to be laid out on a long sheet
of paper; maybe two feet or longer.**

SENTENCES FOR THE BOARD

1. you let your coat laying on the chair to often

2. sounds of a singing school are one of our favorite songs

---

1. im gonna set on this chair and then i will right a letter

2. mans clothing is sold in that there department over their

---

1. no i hasnt spoke to them yet

2. he was more nice to me then he was to you

---

1. alice and betty have drived four hundred miles today and now theyll rest a few days

2. your bound to meet many people of danish descent in racine wisconsin

---

1. tomorrow the sun will raise at 522 am and we will rise the flag at 600 am

2. life in the vineyards a Magazine article tells about grape production in california

Resource: Short Shots (Language Arts-Practice Sentences), J.M. Enterprises, Inc., Box 488, Bel Air, MD 21014, 1981 James A. Kleman, #ISBNO-938464-10-8,Copyright Reserved.

Lesson 4	5	6	7	8	9	10	11	12	13
dream	dropped	hopped	knew	threw	chewed	drew	drawn	lawn	raw
blew	flew	grew	walked	talking	draw	paw	fault	daughter	
blue	sweet	sweetest	lost	costs	cross	pause	tallest		
firemen	sweat	sweater	stood	football	looked	football			
before	brushing	wood	could	should	picked				
nobody	such	would	zoom	too	lunchroom				
when	beginning	classroom	mixes	two	falling	couldn't	shouldn't	won't	
meat	ever	fixes	quick	to	trucks	fighting	highway		
meet	very	cracked	Paul	chicken					
done	every	wanted	don't	claw					
sweep	then	can't	who's	where's	what's				
twine	tricks	here's	once	never					
went	lunch	kind	haven't	weren't	wouldn't				
want	thanked	aren't	I'd	they'd					
our	special	guesses	necktie						
hour	pie		write						
swift		bite	right	brightest	lighthouse				
gives		fight	calling	cause	because				
twist		wild	jaw	caught	taught				
answered		sign							

Dear Mom and Dad,

May I have a new bottle of <u>glue</u>? I need it for my

first grade work.

Thank you!

Love,

_____

- -

Dear Mom and Dad,

May I have a new <u>pencil</u>? I need it for my first

grade work.

Thank you!

Love,

_____

25 ...	100%	20 ...	100%	15 ...	100%	5 ...	100%
24 ...	96%	19 ...	95%	14 ...	93%	4 ...	80%
23 ...	92%	18 ...	90%	13 ...	87%	3 ...	60%
22 ...	88%	17 ...	85%	12 ...	80%	2 ...	40%
21 ...	84%	16 ...	80%	11 ...	73%	1 ...	20%
20 ...	80%	15 ...	75%	10 ...	67%		
19 ...	76%	14 ...	70%	9 ...	60%		
18 ...	72%	13 ...	65%	8 ...	53%		
16 ...	64%	12 ...	60%	7 ...	47%		
15 ...	60%	11 ...	55%	6 ...	40%		
14 ...	56%	10 ...	50%	5 ...	33%		
13 ...	52%	9 ...	45%	4 ...	27%		
12 ...	48%	8 ...	40%	3 ...	20%		
11 ...	44%	7 ...	35%	2 ...	13%		
10 ...	40%	6 ...	30%	1 ...	7%		
9 ...	36%	5 ...	25%				
8 ...	32%	4 ...	20%				
7 ...	28%	3 ...	15%				
6 ...	24%	2 ...	10%				
5 ...	20%	1 ...	5%				
4 ...	16%						
3 ...	12%						
2 ...	8%						
1 ...	4%						

LESSON PLAN

Lesson Topic: Date: Grade:

Learner Outcome: Teacher:

Materials Used:

Evaluation:

Lesson Design:

Anticipatory Set:

Objective:

Input:

Modeling:

Check for Understanding:

Guided Practice:

Independent Practice:

Closure

Evaluation/Changes for next time?

| Birds Fly, Bears Don't | Level 5   p. 1 |

- Introduce Book and Skill Pack - Refer to Table of Contents

- TE 2-3   Introduce Unit 1: A Little Work, A Little Play

- TE 8-9   Introduce "A Fish Out of Water" pp. 8-11

  Vocabulary: Swimming, was, of, another, beautiful, yesterday, say, you'll, it's

  Skillpack p. 1 (vocabulary)

- TE 10-13 Guided reading for pp. 8-11

- TE 14   Focus on Comprehension

- TE 15   Reality/Fantasy

  Skillpack p. 2 (reality, fantasy)

- TE 16   Vowel Digraphs: ai, ay, ea, short o, i with magic e

  Skillpack p. 3 (o, i __ e, ai, ay, ea

  Consonant digraphs and blends: ck, br, cr, dr, fr, gr, pr, tr

  Skillpack p. 4 (blends)

- TE 17   Consonant digraphs and final l, f, ll

  Skillpack p. 5 (final l, f, ll)

- TE 20   Introduce: "A Day With Grandpa" pp. 12-17

  Vocabulary: great, you, all, listen, talk, saw, stop, as

  Skillpack p. 6 (vocabulary)

- TE 21-27 Guided reading for pp. 12-17

- TE 27   Focus on Comprehension

- TE 28-29 Reality, Fantasy

      Skillpack p. 7 (reality, fantasy)

      Contractions with is, not, will (Review)

      Skillpack p. 8 (contractions)

- TE 30   Inflections ____s, and ____ing

      Consonant blends -- st (initial and final)

      Skillpack p. 9 (st)

- TE 32   Short u

      Skillpack p. 10 (u)

- TE 33   Consonant digraphs: l, ll, ff

      Skillpack p. 11 (l, ll, ff)

- TE 35   Poem: Grandpa pp. 18-19

- TE 38   Introduce: "And I Mean It, Stanley" pp. 20-25

      Vocabulary: care, fence, know, making, Stanley, ever, aw, stay, best, well neat

      Skillpack p. 12 (vocabulary)

- TE 40-45 Guided reading for pp. 20-25

- TE 46-47 Reality - fantasy

      Skillpack p. 13 (reality, fantasy)

- TE 47   Inflections: ____ed, ____s, ____ING

      Skillpack p. 14 (____ed)

- TE 48   Compound Words

      Skillpack p. 15 (compound words)

- TE 49   Decoding with "st"
      Skillpack p. 16 (st)

RECORDING STUDENT JOBS IN COOPERATIVE LEARNING

DATE	1/2	1/9	1/16	1/23	1/30	2/6	2/13	2/20	2/27	3/6	3/13	3/20	3/2
Brian	R	P-E	S-C										
Stephanie	P-E	S-C	R										
Jeff	S-C	R	P-E										

R = Recorder   E = Encourager   P = Prober   C = Checker

171

MONDAY
Teacher's Edition_____

Children's Book_____

Workbook_____

Ditto Sheets_____

Other Work_____

TUESDAY
Teacher's Edition_____

Children's Book_____

Workbook_____

Ditto Sheets_____

Other Work_____

WEDNESDAY
Teacher's Edition_____

Children's Book_____

Workbook_____

Ditto Sheets_____

Other Work_____

THURSDAY
Teacher's Edition_____

Children's Book_____

Workbook_____

Ditto Sheets_____
Other Work_____

FRIDAY
Teacher's Edition_____

Children's Book_____

Workbook_____

Ditto Sheets_____
Other Work_____

- REFERENCES -

Oral Presentation Strategies
by Loretta Brandt Minn

- REFERENCES -

FALL TIME SAVERS
Susan Schumann Nowlin

Monthly "Must-Haves" for March and April from Instructional Fair

MARCH

IF311   Hot Air Balloons - Put 'Em Ups
IF362   Hot Air Balloons - Individual Incentive Crafts
IF366   Balloons! Balloons! - Individual Incentive Crafts
IF607   Women in American History - Teaching Poster Set
IF707   Teacher Humor Notes - Cards from a Teacher
IF809   Women in American History - 20 Questions
IF875   Women in American History - Puzzles/1587-1875
IF876   Women in American History - Puzzles/1840-1930
IF877   Women in American History - Puzzles/1900-1960
IF878   Women in American History - Puzzles/1950-Present
IF1803   Nutrition Grades. 3-4 - DUplicating Book
IF2003   Balloons - Special Value Package
IF4207   Windy Days - Reward Seals
IF4229   A Bit O' Irish - Reward Seals
IF4267   Critters n' Balloons - Circle Reward Seals
IF4314   Hot Air Balloons - Chart Seals
IF8561   Arts & Crafts Grades, 1-3 - Resource Book
IF8562   Arts & Crafts Grades. 4-6 - Resource Book
IF8607   Lambs, Lions & Leprechauns - March Holiday Kit

APRIL

IF248   Rainbows & Butterflies - Personal Reward Sear Charts
IF253   Book Report - Personal Reward Seal Charts
IF290   Bookworm Club - Contest Chart
IF295   Rainbows & Butterflies - Put 'Em Ups
IF356   Spring - Individual Incentive Charts
IF361   Butterflies - Individual Incentive Charts
IF367   Rainbows & Butterflies - Individual Incentive Charts
IF368   We Love Reading - Individual Incentive Charts
IF1079   Math Practice Level 1 - Big Value Book
IF1080   Math Practice Level 2 - Big Value Book
IF1081   Math Practice Level 3 - Big Value Book
IF1082   Math Practice Level 4 - Big Value Book
IF1083   Math Practice Level 5 - Big Value Book
IF1084   Math Practice Level 6 - Big Value Book
IF1085   Math Practice Levels 6-8 - Big Value Book
IF2011   Rainbows & Butterflies - Special Value Package
IF2803   Basic Library Skills Grades. 2-3 - Duplicating Book
IF2804   Using Library Skills Grades. 4-6 - Duplicating Book
IF4009   Rainbows & Butterflies - Reward Seals

(Continued on back of sheet)

IF4016   Spring & Easter - Reward Seals
IF4018   Mr. Readmore - Reward Seals
IF4208   Spring Time - Reward Seals
IF4220   Great Rainbows - Reward Seals
IF4230   Bunnies 'n Eggs - Reward Seals
IF4231   Bright Butterflies - Reward Seals
IF4274   Spring - Circle Reward Seals
IF4304   Rainbows & Butterflies - Chart Seals
IF4324   Bright Books - Chart Seals
IF4413   I'm Hooked on Books - Wear 'Em Badges
IF4422   Reading Stars - Wear 'Em Badges
IF8608   Spring/April Holiday Kit
IF0114-0165   I Love Reading - Homework Booklet Series

- REFERENCES -

THE INSTRUCTOR BIG BOOK SERIES

Big Idea Book --- 750 best classroom do-it and use-its from INSTRUCTOR magazine. **IB401**
Big Basics Book --- 55 master plans for teaching the basics, with over 100 reproducibles. **IB402**
Big Holiday Book --- Seasonal Songs, stories, poems, plays, and art, plus an activities calendar. **IB403**
Big Seasonal Arts & Crafts Book --- Over 300 projects for special days and seasons. **IB404**
Big Language Arts Book for Primary Grades -- 136 readings and language skills reproducibles. **IB405**
Big Math Book for Primary Grades --- 135 Reproducibles on number concepts and processes. **IB406**
Big Book of Teacher Savers -- Class lists, letters to parents, record-keeping forms, calendars, maps, writing forms, and more. **IB407**
Synonyms, Sentences, and Spelling Bees: Language Skills Book A -- Over 140 reproducibles. **IB408**
Periods, Paragraphs, and Prepositions: Language Skills Book B -- OVer 140 reproducibles. **IB409**
Big Book of Reading Ideas -- Teacher-tested reading ideas for use with any reading system. **IB410**
Teacher's Activity Calendar -- Red- letter days, ideas, units, for the school year. **IB411**
Early Education Almanac -- Hundreds of activities for kindergarten and beyond. **IB412**
Paper, Pen, and Think -- Ideas galore for developing a sequential writing program. **IB413**
Bearing the Bulletin Board Blues -- Step-by-step ways to bulletin board learning centers. **IB414**
Success with Sticky Subjects -- Books A and B together offer over 240 reproducible worksheets for classroom drill in problem areas of the curriculum. **Book A -- IB415. Book B -- IB416.**
Foolproof, Failsafe Seasonal Science -- Units, experiments, exploration, and quick activities. **IB417**
Poetry Place Anthology -- 605 favorite poems from INSTRUCTOR organized for instant access. **IB418**
Big Book of Plays -- 82 original, reproducible plays for all occasions and levels. **IB419**
Artfully Easy! -- "How-to" workshops on teaching art basics, group projects, and much more! **IB420**
Big Book of Study Skills -- Techniques and activities for the basic subject areas. **IB421**
Big Book of Study Skills Reproducibles -- Over 125 classroom-tested worksheets for all levels. **B422**
Big Book of Computer Activities -- A hands-on guide for using computers in every subject. **IB423**
Read-Aloud Anthology -- 98 stories for all grades and all occasions. **IB424**
Page-a-Day-Pursuits -- Over 300 reproducibles on famous days, birthdays, and events. **IB425**
Big Book of Holidays Word Puzzles -- Over 400 skill-builders for 130 year 'round celebrations. **IB426**
Big Book of Health and Safety -- Reproducibles activities to shape up the health curriculum. **IB427**
Teacher Savers Two -- All new reproducible awards, contracts, letters, sanity-keepers galore. **IB428**
Celebrate America -- Over 200 reproducible activities about the symbols, the land, the people of the U.S.A. Maps, graphs, timelines, folklore, and more. Eight pull-out posters. **IB429**
Big Book of Absolutely Everything -- 1001 ideas to take you through the school year. **IB430**
Language Unlimited -- 160 reproducibles sharpen reading, writing, listening skills. **IB431**
Children and Media -- Activities help kids learn from TV, radio, film, videotape, print. **IB432**
Blockbuster Bulletin Boards -- 366 teacher originals for all grads, subject, and seasons. **IB433**
Hey Gang! Let's Put On A Show -- 50 original skits, choral readings, plays for all ages. **IB434**

Chapter VIII - Bulletin Boards

TEACHER PLEASE NOTE: Please be aware that many of the ideas shared by teachers can and do transcend across several grade levels. Be sure to read all grades' suggestions in order to profit from the many other excellent ideas.

INTRODUCTION

Like it or not, first impressions count and are important. Your room is what students, parents, visitors, and administrators identify with you. Bulletin Boards and the room appearance do reflect upon you.

Students spend a large share of their lifetime in your classroom. Is it bright, attractive, and inviting? Does it foster student pride and motivate interest? Are bulletin boards used for decorative and instructional use? Are students involved in them?

The following ideas shared by teachers may provide you with a few new ideas.

NOTES:

"An ounce of example is worth a ton of advice."

Anonymous

YEAR LONG

Have a **year-long bulletin board** which eliminates redoing it over and over. Divide the space into rectangles with string. Each student has his/her name in one of the spaces. Good work, family pictures, etc. may be spotlighted. Remember to have students change "THEIR" spaces <u>often</u>.

SELF-ESTEEM "FOCUS"

Self-esteem is paramount with a **"Focus"** bulletin board. Each week a different student is in **"Focus."** They bring pictures and things of their own from home to put up. On Friday, the student shares about their board. The class can ask three questions about the student afterward. If you take a picture of the student next to their board, it makes a nice gift at the end of the school year. Perhaps have a student desk next to the bulletin board to display hobbies or collections.

PRIORITY

Spend shorter amounts of time on seasonal "fluff" which normally has a very limited educational value, and invest more in curriculum-orientated themes. It sets a business-like tone and focus.

WORKING BOARD

"Working" bulletin boards are great for stations and open-ended assignments. They provide manipulatives, matching exercises, and pockets to explore and fill. They are easily targeted to specific curriculum areas which reinforce important concepts, skills, and content.
(See example "A", p. 191)

RECOGNITION

Make a **"Boiling Kettle"** display with magic numbers or letters coming out of it. Students see if they can identify the symbol of the day or week. This is especially effective around Halloween.

CREATIVE IDEAS

Make a **"Creative Writing Ideas"** bulletin board for **WRITING** assignment and/or free time. Have 30+ library pockets, each filled with a paper cut out of different animals, people, and objects. Each pocket holds one item and the name of the item is listed in large letters on the pocket. Students select an item to write about, color the item, and glue it on their story. It saves time developing ideas to write about and gives a wide choice.

STUDENT SHARING

Set aside one bulletin board all year for individual students to share about themselves. Put it on a rotating schedule. Each student has one week to display pictures, interests, etc. about themselves. Send a note to parents two weeks before their turn, so the family can be involved. The entire class will get to know each other.

MURALS

A fun, quick, attractive space filler for above windows, bulletin boards, and blank walls can be accomplished by assigning groups a mural. Holidays, seasons, current studies, and their choice make good topics.

NUMBER LINE

A teaching tool is a number line corresponding to a "regular" calendar for comparison. Special days on the **"time line"** should be identified. Talk about today, yesterday, and tomorrow. Take it one step further, by counting the number of days in the school year, by adding <u>one</u> stick in either the 1's, 10's, or 100's can. Also, odd and even numbers can be identified by putting the day's date on a hook labeled odd or even. It is a good opening routine.

TIME LINE CALENDAR

Don't make a new calendar bulletin board every month. Put your calendar on a time line (1-31 days). Attach a string from one end to the other with a bead which can slide to the next date. Use color paper with special events written out, and these can be taped to the chalkboard underneath, pinned on the bulletin board surface, or clipped on with clothespins.

THEME

The teacher supplies large figure shapes and the title. Students fill in the space with their work which relates to the theme. It might become a mosaic of constellations, oceans, clouds, bike safety, bears, letters, etc.

"OUR STICKER CLUB"

Have an **"Our Sticker Club"** bulletin board. Each child has a 5 x 8 inch card with his/her name on it, which is placed on the bulletin board. He/she puts one reward sticker on it each day. At the end of the month the students take their cards home to show their family.

"WACKY WEDNESDAY"

For a mid-week diversion, have a **"Wacky Wednesday."** Each student shares a joke, writes it out, and puts it on the **Wacky Wednesday Bulletin Board**. Research for them in the library.

FUTURE ARTIST

Show student "ownership" of the room with a **"Future Artist"** bulletin board. Any child can put up any art work at anytime. It can be an art project or their own free drawings.

STUDENT TAKE DOWN

Have responsible students carefully take down bulletin boards when finished. This can save untold minutes in staple removal by yours truly.

OLDER STUDENT HELP

Primary teachers...ask the intermediate teachers for a responsible student to do some cutting or opaque drawing for your bulletin boards. Delegate whenever possible.

OPAQUE

Opaque large figures and have students color them when finished with assigned work. Coloring books work well for this. The finished pictures make excellent room or hall decorations.

"You need to spend time to gain time in most areas of education."

Ruth Morgan

NOTES;

"Whether you think you can or whether you think you can't, you're right."

Henry Ford

"NEW YEAR RESOLUTION

Do a **"New Year Resolution"** bulletin board. Take down after a few weeks and carefully save. Reread them to the class during the last week of school. See how the new goals are coming along. Don't forget to put your own down.

VISUAL BEHAVIOR

A display of moveable students' names, on a discipline bulletin board, can give a quick visual as to who is not finished with work, has a warning for an infraction, or is on top of things and can be chosen for something special. Themes can be a mountain with **"Stay on Top of Things,"** (names on mountain climbers), or an ugly spider in a web with **"Stay Out of the Web,"** (names on butterflies), or a ship with names on swords saying **"Stay Off the Plank."**

INFORMATION

Establish an **"information board."** Post a permanent calendar, daily schedule reminders for the day/week, computer lab schedule, field trip date, etc. This will eliminate the need for students to continually ask you for dates and times for upcoming events.

ANNOUNCE-MENTS

Have an **"Announcement Board."** Any parent or student can get an extra copy of handouts, if they should lose theirs. They do not have to come to ask you for something. Just always run an extra 3-5 copies. It is a good place to display schedules, special classes, and upcoming events to remember.

CURRENT NEWS

A working bulletin board labeled **"Current News"** provides for daily discussion of important news events. Divide it into fourths, and label them local, state, national, and world. Global education, speaking in front of a group, critical thinking skills, reading, and other learner outcomes are integrated into a meaningful lesson, on a regular basis, without any time spent on lesson planning. Change the newspaper articles regularly.

GROUP ASSIGNMENT

Divide one large bulletin board area up into 4-6 areas. Assign groups of students to develop their own area into a display about a current area of study. Perhaps each group could take a separate section of a certain unit instead of the same topic. Energy could have oil, water, electric, muscle, heat, gas, chemical, etc.

NOTES:

"Education is learning what you didn't even know you didn't know."

--Daniel J. Boorstin
Democracy and Its Discontents (Random House)

STUDENT GROUPS	Assign students by groups to do a bulletin board once per month. The board may be seasonal, theme or unit orientated, a learning quiz-type board, or students' choice. They get the experience and fun of making the room a better place, while you enjoy using the time better spent in another area.
COOPERATIVE PROJECT	Assign a cooperative project, to several students, to design a bulletin board, and put it up. It teaches them how to organize, plan, and work together; plus freeing up time for the teacher in a constructive manner.
CONTEST	Set up a contest, between groups of students, as to which group can come up with the best bulletin board idea. Creative thinking and cooperative learning are a few advantages of this set up. The winners get to put up their bulletin board when their work is completed, before, or after school.
NEWS BOARD	Use one bulletin board space for a **"News Bulletin Board."** Students bring in articles to discuss for current events, and post them for a few days at a time. Include who, what, when, where, why, and how in the reports.
INFORMATION	Set aside one bulletin board area for an **"Assignment Board."** Label down the left side with the subject areas. Label across the top with the days of the week for a month or more. Write in all assignments, as they are made or even ahead of time if students are that self-directed. It saves a lot of questions, and there is no excuse for not knowing the assignment.
"QUOTES"	Have a weekly motto or saying. Post it on the **"Quote"** bulletin board. Discuss its meaning and refer to it throughout the week. Affirmations and attitudes are coupled with positive **"words to live by."** Soon you will start hearing the students using these quotes in their normal conversation.
TRIVIA QUESTIONS	Encourage the use of research and reference books with a **"Trivia Questions"** bulletin board. Change the questions each week. Do in spare time or give extra credit, as you wish.

PICTURES OF STUDENTS

Take photographs of your students when they are doing different projects. Rotate the pictures each month, but keep them for the end of the year. At the end of the year, give all the pictures away to the students to enjoy the remembrances.

STUDENTS' WORK

Use more student work on bulletin boards. It gives purpose for doing their work well, establishes good P.R. when parent visitors come, saves teacher time in planning and making the displays, and most importantly provides a climate of student ownership in the room.

WORLD NEWS

A **"World News"** bulletin board, using a world map and yarn, is used to locate current event locations by connecting the articles to the correct place on the map with yarn and pins.

"Common sense is not so common."

Volatire

RECORD YOUR BOARDS

Take colored pictures of your own bulletin boards and other teachers' bulletin boards. Keep them in plastic picture pockets, for easy reference, by subject. Always take a camera when visiting other schools to get that special idea down on film.

TODAY'S WORD

To help develop student vocabulary, plan for a daily word of emphasis and post it on the **"Today's Word"** bulletin board. Review yesterday's and post today's. Discussion will show its importance, what it means, and where it can be used.

MONTHLY WORDS

Establish a bulletin board entitled **"Monthly Words."** It is their job to use these in as many ways as they can, such as handwriting, spelling, talking, creative writing, etc. They are taken from the season, holiday, special school events, unit themes, daily happenings, etc.

CLOTH

Use bright colored cloth for the total background of the bulletin boards. There is no fading of paper and staples, thumbtacks, or pinholes do not show. Leave them up all summer, too. They are ready to go in the fall.

NON-FADE BACKGROUND

Use background colors that do not fade as fast. Blue is the worst. Yellow and white last longer and can be reused more often, eliminating the need to reback your boards so often. Purchase large rolls of corrugated cardboard paper for backgrounds. It can be reused.

POSTERS

Posters provide a purposeful focus while at the same time filing up a lot of space; this is especially useful, at the beginning of the year, before student work starts coming in and when time is of an essence.

LETTERING

Save time by not putting up individual letters. Just glue them to colored construction paper strips and put up a word or a phrase at a time. The letters last much longer, also.

EXTRAS

Always cut extras of everything while you are making your bulletin board letters and designs. That way, if something gets lost or torn you will always have a ready backup.

LAMINATE Laminate, or cover colored paper with contact paper, before cutting out those letters or designs for your bulletin boards. This will extend the life of your product many times over. Die cut your materials if you have a die cutter available.

STORAGE Keep each bulletin board's materials in a large plastic bag for reuse, attaching a sketch of its layout for easy identification and setup. Keep generic files for different sized and shaped letters, numbers, and for different types of borders.

STORAGE Build your bulletin boards in pieces so that they fit into drawers. Storage is easier and durability is lengthened. Have the drawers labeled as to the months the materials will be used.

FELT LETTERS Cut letters out of thin, stiff felt. The vivid colors do not fade, and pinholes do not show even after years of use. Cut several of each letter and vary the colors and size.

STARRED PAPERS A permanent bulletin board might be one for **"Starred Papers"** on display. These spotlighted papers should be for **"most improved"** as well as top grades. Could these students line up first for lunch and recess?

BLOW-UP PICTURES Use the opaque projector to "blow up" the pictures larger than life. Get older students to do the tracing and coloring. The finished product makes them feel like successful artists. Let them sign them.

YOUR OWN BOARD Put your desk by **"your"** own bulletin board. Use it for important papers, bulletins, notices, student-made notes, family pictures, check-off lists, etc.--be creative. These things will be visible and at your fingertips. It will be well-used wall space and close enough to save you many steps. Hang your fly swatter on it.

WORKING BOARDS Use more **"working bulletin boards."** These provide the basic format, after which the students do the manipulating and filling in of objects and spaces.

STUDENT HELP Have students put up and take down all their own work. This makes them feel important and helps with fine motor development. There is always higher interest in their own work, than a teacher-made bulletin board.

VOLUNTEERS Have a volunteer, parent/guardian, educational aide, or a student teacher put up your bulletin board displays. A sketch or picture, along with the premade materials, should be all you need to supply. Think of the time this will save!

DIVIDED WORKLOAD Team teachers may divide up the responsibility by the number of bulletin boards per teacher. Take turns doing them in "common" areas. Try to develop **"instructional"** designs so that the subjects match the units being taught. This is especially helpful for the "visual" learner's memory.

STUDENT TEACHER BOARD Assign a student teacher to make a bulletin board. Whatever it is, it should be reusable so that they keep it, and it will save them time in their own classroom the next year.

K-ROY LETTERING BOARD Use a K-roy Lettering Machine for a variety of crisp, professional applications. Can be purchased from

> **Tierney**
> **2505 University Avenue**
> **St. Paul, Minnesota 55114**
> **(612) 647-1600**

It prints out a variety of items and sizes to label things on a bulletin board.

"PRINT SHOP" Use a computer program, such as **"Print Shop,"** to make headings and banners for your bulletin boards. They are fast, fresh, neat, and can even be colored by students prior to their use. Print Shop runs on an Apple GS. A color printer ribbon is even more advantageous.

ADDITIONAL IDEAS Check your public library, school district's professional library, your school's library, and book stores for many ideas that would fit perfectly into your plans.

PURCHASE IDEAS A fine bulletin board idea books is:

> **Blockbuster Bulletin Boards #IB433**
> Instructor Books
> 545 5th Avenue
> New York, NY 10017

It has 366 teacher originals for all grades, subjects and seasons.

LETTERS Sets of letters may be purchased for less than $5.00 from
St. Paul Book and Stationary Store
1233 West County Road E
St. Paul, MN 55112

DIE CUT Use a Die Cutting machine to make multiple copies of
FOR designs for the number of the days in a month. For
CALENDARS example, stamp out 31 evergreen trees for December's
calendar. It sure beats cutting them out by hand. Simply file
them and use over each year. **Idea: Laminate the paper
before you die cut for longer durability.**

FRAME Use magic marker to mark off permanent, equal, spaces, a
STUDENTS' little larger than the size of a piece of paper. Use to display
WORK students' work. The marks act as a frame. Since they are
flat, just cover it up with another backing when not used for
this purpose.

YARN SPACES Yarn, stretched from one pin to another, marks off nice
straight lines or squares on a bulletin board. It is colorful,
three dimensional, and attractive.

REWARD When all assignments are completed, students can choose to
work on a bulletin board as a reward.

SPECIFIC Put bulletin boards on your priority list to do the last week of
GOAL each month. Specifying this goal, will give you a fresh start,
and a new outlook on the beginning of each month.
Following themes of the season is a natural and you won't
get that feeling of being behind.

WORKING BOARD

Desert	Natural Resources	Plant Life	People How They Live
Painted	Student Responses	Student Responses	Student Responses
Arabian	''	''	''
Majove	''	''	''
Sahara	''	''	''

WORKING BOARD

Desert	Natural Resources	Plant Life	People How They Live
Painted			
Arabian			
Majove			
Sahara			